# It Happened in
# AMERICA

# It Happened in AMERICA

## TRUE STORIES FROM THE FIFTY STATES

★ ★ ★

## LILA PERL

### Illustrated by Ib Ohlsson

HENRY HOLT AND COMPANY ★ NEW YORK

*To Brenda Bowen*
*who made it happen*
*—L. P.*

*To Ria*
*—I. 0.*

★

Text copyright © 1992 by Lila Perl
Illustrations copyright © 1992 by Ib Ohlsson
All rights reserved.
Published in Canada by Fitzhenry & Whiteside Ltd.,
195 Allstate Parkway, Markham, Ontario L3R 4T8.

Library of Congress Cataloging-in-Publication Data
Perl, Lila.
It happened in America: true stories from the fifty states /
Lila Perl; illustrations by Ib Ohlsson.
Includes bibliographical references.
Summary: Presents historical anecdotes from each of the fifty states,
with an emphasis on women and ethnic minorities.
1. United States—History—Anecdote—Juvenile literature.
2. Minorities—United States—History—Anecdotes—Juvenile literature.
[1. United States—History.]   I. Ohlsson, Ib, ill.   II. Title.
E178.3.P47   1992        973'—dc20        92-6742

ISBN 0-8050-1719-4 (hardcover)
3   5   7   9   10   8   6   4
ISBN 0-8050-4707-7 (paperback)
1   3   5   7   9   10   8   6   4   2
First published in hardcover in 1992
by Henry Holt and Company, Inc.
First paperback edition, 1996
Printed in the United States of America on acid-free paper.∞

# CONTENTS

# CONTENTS ★ ix

# ★ Acknowledgments ★

*The author is grateful to the following individuals
and institutions for helpful information and materials:*

Amana Colonies Convention and Visitors Bureau,
Amana, Iowa
Arkansas Historical Association, Fayetteville, Arkansas
Circus World Museum, Baraboo, Wisconsin
Craig Claiborne
Dinosaur National Monument, Utah/Colorado
Little White House Historic Site, Warm Springs, Georgia
Mammoth Cave National Park, Mammoth Cave, Kentucky
Missouri Historical Society, St. Louis, Missouri
Montana Historical Society, Helena, Montana
Parker Brothers, Beverly, Massachusetts
Sharlot Hall Historical Society, Prescott, Arizona
Laurin Stamm, Foods Editor, *Vicksburg Evening Post,*
Vicksburg, Mississippi
Star-Spangled Banner Flag House, Baltimore, Maryland
Studebaker National Museum, South Bend, Indiana
Mary Frances Terry, Delta Point River Restaurant,
Vicksburg, Mississippi
Sheri Walter, Queens Borough Public Library
Washington State Historical Society, Tacoma, Washington

*and
special thanks for
research and technical assistance
to
Diane Hocking*

# ★ It Happened in America ★

Crisscrossing the United States from Maine to Hawaii, from Alaska to Florida, from north to south and east to west, we make an amazing discovery. America is a storybook.

Its pages are crammed with tales of quiet courage and dashing bravado, feats of accomplishment and magnificent failures. There are sad stories and funny stories, rollicking yarns and touching anecdotes. They come out of every period of history, beginning with the precolonial world of the Native Americans, and they are still happening today. America's stories also reflect the lives of Europeans and Africans, Asians and Hispanics, Middle Easterners and Polynesians, transplanted to its shores. The stories told in this book offer a rich sampling of the varied peoples of each of the fifty states. And all of them are true.

Where do these true stories come from? They come from the truths at the heart of America's folklore and legends. They come out of the private, hand-scrawled diaries of little-known citizens and out of the more formal writings of famous figures. They come out of history books and biographies that go behind the scenes and dig into the everyday experiences of Alaska gold miners and Idaho mountain men, Yankee peddlers and Hawaiian royalty, Texas cowhands and the immigrant pioneers of the Midwest and the Great Plains.

The character of each region of the country is highlighted by the true stories from each of it states. From New England, for example, we learn about Martha Ballard, a midwife and healer, who trekked through the snows and mud of the Maine backcountry of the late 1700s to bring aid and comfort to her neighbors.

On the Middle Atlantic seaboard, we watch Pennsylvania Germans design and build the Conestoga wagon—otherwise known as the prairie schooner—that was to take families all the way to the shores of the Pacific.

Traveling to the South, we find out about a lonely, abandoned Chinese orange-grower who helped Florida make its mark in the citrus industry, and about the flamboyant pirate Jean Lafitte, who helped save Louisiana from the British in the Battle of New Orleans. We also trace the struggle of African-Americans for freedom and equality, from the failed crusade of Denmark Vesey to the historic bus ride of Rosa Parks.

In the Midwest, we follow the route of black fugitive slaves on Ohio's Underground Railroad and look in on the Kellogg brothers of Battle Creek, Michigan, as they concoct the first successful batch of their ready-to-eat breakfast cereal.

The Rocky Mountain states, we discover, aren't famous only for wilderness survival and the unearthing of dinosaur bones. Wyoming gave women the vote while it was still a territory, and Montana sent the first female representative to the United States Congress.

In the Southwest, we learn how it happened that camels from Arabia once walked the desert trails of Arizona. In the Pacific region, we accompany a group of "forty-niners" trapped in California's Death Valley, who were lucky indeed to escape its terrors, leaving behind everything *but* their lives.

Each story is preceded by a brief look at the history, geographical features, naming, peopling, and economy of the state. Some stories are harrowing and daring, others lighthearted and humorous, or romantic and adventurous. But we can proudly say of each of these fifty stories . . . it happened in America.

# ★ ★ ★ A Map of the ★ ★ ★
# United States of America

A D A

NEW HAMPSHIRE
VERMONT
MAINE
MASSACHUSETTS
WISCONSIN
NEW YORK
MICHIGAN
PENNSYLVANIA
RHODE ISLAND
CONNECTICUT
★ WASHINGTON, D.C.
OHIO
W.
INDIANA
VIRGINIA
NEW JERSEY
ILLINOIS
KENTUCKY
VIRGINIA
DELAWARE
NORTH
CAROLINA
MARYLAND
TENNESSEE
SOUTH
CAROLINA
MISSISSIPPI
GEORGIA
ALABAMA
Atlantic
Ocean
FLORIDA
Gulf of Mexico

# ALABAMA

The Alibamu, a Creek Indian people, gave Alabama its name. *Alibamu* means "clearers of the thickets," for the Indians of the area were tireless gatherers of a kind of holly plant from which they brewed a potent drink. One of Alabama's nicknames is *The Cotton State*. Cotton was its main crop from the early 1800s until 1910, when an insect called the boll weevil appeared and destroyed most of it.

This disaster alerted farmers to the need for diversity; they branched out into the growing of corn, hay, fruits, sweet potatoes, pecans, and especially peanuts. Slave-born George Washington Carver won lasting fame for his agricultural research at Alabama's Tuskegee Institute, where he developed over three hundred industrial products from the peanut alone.

BOLL WEEVIL

Alabama was wrested from the Creek and other crop-raising Indians by a succession of Spanish explorers, French traders, and English settlers. It was admitted to the Union on December 14, 1819. Like most of the other slave-holding states, Alabama seceded from the Union in 1861 and suffered from the ravages of the Civil War and its aftermath.

In the mid-1950s, Alabama was the scene of two early milestones in the struggle for civil rights. Dr. Martin Luther King, Jr., came forward to lead the protest against segregated seating on Montgomery city buses, and Autherine Lucy became the first black student to enroll in the all-white University of Alabama.

---

**Question**: Which state built a monument to a quarter-inch-long beetle with a sharp snout?

**Answer**: Alabama. The Boll Weevil Monument was erected in the town of Enterprise, in 1919. Carved on it are the words, "In profound appreciation of the boll weevil and what it has done as the herald of prosperity."

---

# The Day Rosa Parks Said No to "Jim Crow"

"Jim Crow" wasn't the name of a real person. It was an unflattering term used to describe someone who was "black as a crow." As far back as the 1820s, long before the Civil War, white entertainers used to blacken their faces and perform jokes, songs, and dances in minstrel shows. "Jim Crow" was the name of one of the song-and-dance acts.

From 1861 to 1865, Americans of the North and the South were locked in the terrible struggle of the Civil War. When the war ended, the United States became a single nation once again and slavery was abolished throughout the land. But Jim Crow managed to live on.

Starting in the 1880s, the term came to mean the separation of whites and blacks in all sorts of public places. There were separate rest rooms and drinking fountains, separate schools for black and white children, separate waiting rooms at train stations and separate railroad cars to ride in. Restaurants serving whites would not serve black customers. Factories that employed black workers as well as white ones sent blacks around to a special window to collect their pay. And the black water fountains, railroad cars, schools, and other facilities were always shabby and inferior to those used by whites.

One of the most unfair of the Jim Crow practices in the South was the rule forcing black people to ride in the rear section on public buses. The front of the bus was marked off for white riders only. Even if there wasn't a single white rider, no black person was allowed to sit in the "white section."

Even worse was the rule that, if the bus was crowded, white riders had the right to sit in the black section as well. Also, a black could not share a seat with a white, or even sit across the aisle from any white rider. So if a white person took *one* seat in the "black section," three blacks had to get up and stand, squeezing as far into the back of the bus as possible.

Until a wintry Thursday evening late in 1955, only a small number of black people had challenged this and other Jim Crow practices. Those who did faced arrest, and even a beating or more serious form of attack from certain white groups. But on this particular evening, which happened to be December 1, a black woman named Rosa Parks climbed aboard a city bus in Montgomery, Alabama, and took a seat in the forward part of the black section.

Rosa Parks was a bespectacled, forty-two-year-old seamstress who worked in a downtown Montgomery department store doing altera-tions on articles of clothing that didn't fit the customers properly. She had also been doing some Christmas shopping for her family, and she was laden with packages and very tired. After a couple of stops the bus became crowded and, as usual, the black passengers had to start giving up their seats to whites. Rosa Parks sat there quietly until her turn came. But when the white bus driver ordered her to leave her seat, she matter-of-factly answered, "No."

ROSA PARKS

The passengers, black and white, watched tensely as the order was repeated and Rosa Parks refused to budge. She knew she was defying an entrenched rule of the bus company. But something inside her protested strongly. She had simply grown tired of being treated as a second-class citizen everywhere she turned. It just wasn't fair. And it wasn't legal according to the Constitution of the United States.

Rosa Parks was, of course, taken off the bus by the police, arrested, photographed and fingerprinted, and placed in a jail cell. Luckily, someone immediately reported the incident to Edgar Daniel Nixon, a black community leader in Montgomery who had long been fighting for equal rights.

Within a few hours Nixon raised the one hundred dollars necessary to get Rosa Parks out of jail until she would have to appear in court. He also came up with an idea. Over seventy percent of Montgomery's bus riders were black. Suppose they all got together and refused to ride the buses to work, to school, or to anywhere else on the following Monday, December 5. Perhaps some white riders would join in too. The bus company would lose money, for the buses would ride almost empty!

That weekend, meetings were held, leaflets were handed out, and black ministers urged churchgoers to support the boycott—the refusal to ride the buses in order to show their disapproval of one of the many Jim Crow practices.

Sparked by the courage of Rosa Parks, the boycott on Monday, December 5, was an enormous success. Martin Luther King, then a young minister and civil-rights leader, came to the forefront of the movement. People simply walked to school or work, no matter how early they had to get up or how far they had to go, and they cheered as the buses rode by empty. That day Montgomery, Alabama, became "the walking city."

Of course, one day wasn't enough to bring the bus company to its knees. The company was determined to hold out. So were the people of Montgomery. Through the winter, spring, summer, and fall of 1955–56, people walked. They also organized car pools, they bicycled, they traveled in horse-drawn wagons, they even rode on the backs of mules. But most of all, they walked.

Some white people threw stones and bottles at the boycotters. And on the evening of January 30, 1956, Martin Luther King's home in Montgomery was bombed. His family narrowly escaped injury. This

incident brought numerous out-of-state reporters and photographers to Montgomery, and the protest began to receive national attention.

Rosa Parks continued to play her own important role, one that would earn her the name "the mother of the civil-rights movement." A few days after her arrest, she appeared in court, was found guilty of not giving up her seat, and was fined ten dollars, which she refused to pay. She then took steps to bring her case before the Supreme Court, the highest court in the nation. And, finally, on November 13, 1956, nearly a year after her arrest, the Supreme Court ruled that segregated, or separate, seating on buses was unconstitutional.

There was still a long way to go in ridding the nation of the Jim Crow "laws" that created ugly and dangerous feelings in both blacks and whites. But as a result of Rosa Parks's historic bus ride—and the way people in Montgomery, Alabama, banded together despite many hardships—one of them had been struck down forever.

# ALASKA

Alaska takes its name from an Aleutian word meaning "great land." Alaska *is* great, for it is more than twice the size of Texas, the largest state of the lower forty-eight. Five Alaskas would equal the size of the rest of the United States. The "great land" also has the highest mountain in North America—Mount McKinley, also called Denali (20,320 feet)—and a glacier that is bigger than the state of Rhode Island. Even though nearly a third of Alaska lies above the Arctic Circle, it isn't all snow and ice. Summer temperatures in parts of the interior can reach a hundred degrees Fahrenheit, and during the long, sunshiny days strawberries can grow to the size of teacups.

Alaska's earliest inhabitants included the Inuit of the central and northern sections, the Inuit-related Aleuts of the southwestern peninsula and the islands, and the Tlingit and Haida Indians of the southeast. In the 1700s, Russians explored Alaska and set up fur-trapping and fur-trading posts for the Russian czars. Russia sold Alaska to the United States in 1867. The Alaskan gold rush of the late 1800s brought prospectors, settlers, and, in time, the clamor for statehood. Alaska has been nicknamed *The Last Frontier* because, when it finally entered the Union as the forty-ninth state— on January 3, 1959—it was the first new territory on the North American mainland to have been added in forty-seven years.

7

**Question**: Where has the lowest temperature in the United States been recorded?

**Answer**: At a place called Prospect Creek Camp in Alaska. It was 79.8 degrees *below zero* Fahrenheit.

# Ma Pullen and the Chilkoot Pass

"Most terrifically did the wind blow at sixty miles an hour, carrying fine particles of ice and snow in the air, which cut the face almost like glass. The few who tried to be out any length of time would come back with some portion frozen, an ear, cheek, nose or more often the feet . . . and a heavy frost would fringe the eyelashes."

This description of the approach to Alaska's Chilkoot Pass—the gateway to the Klondike gold fields of western Canada—was written in 1898. Less than two years earlier, a fabulous gold strike had been made in the Klondike region. And the most popular route to it was through the Alaskan boom town of Skagway.

At the time of the Klondike gold strike, in the summer of 1896, Skagway wasn't even a town. It was just a place with the name of Cqague, an Indian word, probably of Tlingit origin, for "home of the north wind." Only a single homesteader lived there in a lone cabin. Less than a year later Skagway had over 15,000 people. Filled with *cheechakos*, the Chinook word for "newcomers," it was said to be the largest town in Alaska.

Along with the gold seekers, of course, came the suppliers of food, tools, and camping equipment that would be needed for mining in the far north. Eateries and lodging houses, saloons and dance halls, sprang up. Gamblers, thieves, and other outlaws were all too ready to relieve the newcomers of their money and goods. But the prospectors kept right on coming. The Klondike gold rush, in fact, was more like a stampede.

Not all of Skagway's new residents were out to take unfair advantage of the stampeders. Some of them were honest and helpful businesspeople. One of these was a widow with four sons, known as "Ma" Pullen, who arrived in Skagway in 1897. She was a good cook and set up a tent eatery where she served meals to hungry prospectors passing through town. She also went into the pie-baking business.

But Ma Pullen didn't really consider cooking much of a challenge. There was more money to be made, she figured, in supplying transportation over the terrifying Chilkoot Pass. On the other side of the Pass lay Canada's Yukon Territory and the route to the Klondike. There the Canadian Mounted Police waited to check on the stampeders. Each miner was required by the Canadian government to carry enough food to last a year—about a thousand pounds. In addition, a prospector carried mining equipment, a cookstove, a tent, clothing, and boat-building tools. These easily weighed another thousand pounds.

How was a miner supposed to get over the Chilkoot Pass and onto the Yukon River, which served as a highway north to the Klondike? The strenuous uphill trek through blizzards and icy fogs had to be done in short stages, leaving equipment behind at various relay points. Often it was lost or stolen. Ma Pullen saved her pie-business money and set out to buy pack animals, saddles, and harnesses and to hire local guides. Soon she was the only woman in Skagway in the "packer" business, hauling miners' outfits up the snow- and ice-covered Chilkoot, which because of its rocky outcroppings was actually more passable in winter than in summer. It wasn't surprising that, after a while, Ma Pullen got the notion to set out on a gold stampede of her own. There was a report of a new strike just across the Canadian border, fairly close to Skagway. But shortly after arriving at the gold camp, she broke her arm and decided mining wasn't for her. Ma sensed too that the days of the packing business were numbered—a railway was being built across one of the less steep passes not far from the Chilkoot.

So, sensibly, Ma Pullen went back into the restaurant business in Skagway, and this time she opened a hotel as well. It was two stories high and had an impressive name, the Pullen House. Unlike the tents and raw wooden shacks that served as lodging houses in Skagway, the distinguished Pullen House sat on landscaped grounds dotted with small ponds. It became *the* place to meet for both old-timers and newcomers who could afford a bit of luxury in the wild.

Between 1896 and 1904, the Klondike brought in over a hundred million dollars' worth of gold. But once the most valuable claims had been staked, there was little left for the latecomers. The stampeders began to drift westward along the Yukon River, which flows across the entire main body of Alaska. Soon gold was found in Alaska—at Nome in 1898, and at Fairbanks in 1902. These and other rich strikes were to yield about a billion dollars' worth of Alaskan gold.

Skagway itself began to shrink once the stampede moved west. Today it has a population of under a thousand, and Ma Pullen's hotel is long since gone. But her achievements as a fearless, enterprising frontier woman are ones that Alaskans can point to with pride. Nor has Skagway forgotten "the days of '98." Visitors can stroll along wooden sidewalks in the historic district and can still—weather permitting—hike the Chilkoot Trail in the footsteps of the gold miners of "the last stampede."

ALASKAN MALAMUTE

# ARIZONA

A Papago Indian word, *ari-sonac*, gave Arizona its name. *Ari-sonac* means "small [or a few] springs." This name is fitting, because much of the state is dry and desertlike. One of Arizona's nicknames is *The Grand Canyon State*. The world-famous Grand Canyon is a tremendous gorge slashed by the rushing waters of the Colorado River. The Canyon is over two hundred miles long, as much as eight miles wide from rim to rim, and a mile deep in places. Other Arizona wonders include cactuses that grow as tall as six-story buildings, and the eerie, leafless Petrified Forest. The "forest's" fallen, decayed trees—over a hundred million years old—lie on the ground in broken pieces that have petrified, or gradually turned to colored stone.

Spanish explorers of the 1500s reached this area by journeying north from what is today Mexico. They found cliff-dwelling Indians whose ancestors had arrived at least ten thousand years earlier. Most of present-day Arizona belonged to Spain, and afterward to Mexico; then it was ceded to the United States in 1848, following the Mexican War.

Another nickname for Arizona is *The Baby State*, because it was the last, and therefore the youngest, of the contiguous (meaning physically connected, or touching) forty-eight states. Sometimes it's called *The Valentine State* as well, because it was admitted to the Union on Valentine's Day, February 14, 1912.

13

**Question**: Which state has adopted the blossom of a giant cactus plant as its state flower?

**Answer**: Arizona. The saguaro cactus, which grows in the southern part of the state, may be fifty feet tall, weigh ten tons, or twenty thousand pounds, and live up to two hundred years. In May and June, this largest American cactus produces handsome cream-and-gold flowers.

# Hadji Ali and the Camel Experiment

A caravan of camels laden with goods delicately picks its way across a sandy landscape. Men in turbans and neck scarves ride the camels or walk alongside, guiding them. Sometimes the camel drivers speak sharply to the large beasts, other times they murmur lovingly and even sing to them. Surely we must be watching these stately "ships of the desert" in far-off Arabia or North Africa. But no, we are in the American West. We are in the Arizona territory in the year 1857.

Nobody is quite sure who first had the idea to bring camels to America to help carve out a wagon trail across Arizona for pioneers heading west. It may have been a young lieutenant named Edward Beale, who was assigned to lead the surveying expedition for the United States Army. Or it may have been Jefferson Davis, who in the 1850s was serving in Washington, D.C., as secretary of war.

In any case, in 1856 and again in 1857, the army sent a ship to Egypt and Arabia to buy camels to travel across the rocky, desertlike cactus-lands of Arizona. On board ship the camels had to be tied down in a kneeling position to prevent their tender humps from being bruised as the vessel rolled and heaved on the stormy seas. But both shiploads of camels survived the journey well. Although one camel died on the first voyage, two were born. Altogether, seventy-eight single-humped camels, also known as dromedaries, were landed at a port in Texas, ready to be walked to Arizona to begin their trail breaking.

Along with camels—which had never before been seen in

America—came a handful of men from Egypt and the Arabian peninsula who were experienced in the feeding and watering, packing and driving, of the animals. Among them was one named Hadji Ali.

Hadji Ali had been born in what is now Syria in 1828, and had known and understood camels all his life. The word "Hadji" in his name tells us that he was a devout Muslim who had made the hadj, or religious pilgrimage, from his home in Syria to the holy city of Mecca—birthplace of the prophet Muhammad—in what is today Saudi Arabia.

But the soldiers, scouts, and prospectors of the American West in the mid-1800s knew very little about foreign lands and religions. So they simply slurred "Hadji Ali" into something that sounded like

"Hi Jolly," and that was what they called him. On August 31, 1857, Hadji Ali set out with Lieutenant Beale's "Camel Corps" westward across Arizona.

The expedition included twenty-five camels, eight covered wagons drawn by mules, and about fifty men. As originally hoped, the camels turned out to be excellent pack animals. They could carry much heavier loads than mules could—up to a thousand pounds. They fed on stiff, bitter-tasting desert shrubs, prickly pears, and other spiny cactus varieties. And, unlike the mules, they survived contentedly for days without water.

Each morning Hadji Ali and the other camel drivers arose at three A.M. to pack the camels and be ready to set off by five. Their route across northern Arizona took them through pine forests, mountain snows, and thick mud, as well as dry wastelands. The camels swam rivers and streams and made their way over sharp-edged lava rock and into steep canyons. The widely held belief that the camels' spongy feet would be too tender for stony ground seemed unfounded.

Nearly two months later, on October 18, 1857, the Camel Corps arrived at the Colorado River. Across it lay the state of California. The camels had accomplished their mission. The trail had been opened and the experiment was a success.

Yet within just a few years, almost everyone except Hadji Ali had lost interest in the camels. Lieutenant Beale was given another assignment in 1861, just as the Civil War broke out. And Jefferson Davis left Washington to become the president of the Confederate States of the South, which had seceded from the Union.

Unable to find steady work as a camel driver, Hadji Ali bought several of the camels and loaded them with jugs of fresh water. During the 1860s he could often be found along a stretch of desert road in southwestern Arizona, selling water to thirsty stagecoach passengers headed for California.

Hadji Ali was finally married in 1880, at the age of fifty-two. That same year he became an American citizen and chose the name Philip Tedro for his naturalization certificate. Perhaps he felt that a Spanish rather than an Arabian name was more suitable in the American Southwest. He became the father of two daughters, but somehow he couldn't get used to a settled life. He often took off with a camel train or even a mule train, as a packer, a scout, or a prospector.

Hadji Ali died near the town of Quartzite in southwestern Arizona in 1902. In 1935, the Arizona Highway Department erected a tombstone in the shape of a pyramid—an Egyptian, not a Syrian, monument—over his grave. On the peak of the pyramid, however, stands the figure of a camel to commemorate the role that this adopted son of Arizona played in its development.

What ever happened to the camels themselves, and are there any left in Arizona today? The sellers and drivers of mules were said to have been their worst enemies. Often they turned camels loose on purpose, for they did not know how to handle them and they feared that camels used as pack animals would cut into their livelihood. Some camels were sold to circuses, parks, and zoos. But many became half wild, grazing the land and being shot at by ranchers because their sudden appearance frightened the horses and other livestock.

By 1900 or so the last of the camels and their offspring seemed to have disappeared. Yet for many years afterward, tales were told in Arizona of sighting a camel—or perhaps the ghost of a camel—browsing the scrubby growth in some misty canyon bottom.

# ARKANSAS

Arkansas is named for the Arkansa, or "downstream people," a Sioux Indian group who lived along the Arkansas River near where it flows into the Mississippi. The state's nickname is *The Land of Opportunity*, probably because it is so varied in landscape. People living in the southeastern part of Arkansas might be cotton planters, like their neighbors in Mississippi. In the southwest they might be cattle ranchers, as in nearby Texas. Arkansans who live in the Ozark Mountains of the north often work at forestry and lumbering.

Indians known as Bluff Dwellers who lived in caves in the river cliffs inhabited the region as early as A.D. 500. When Spanish explorers reached the area in the 1500s, Osage, Quapaw, and Caddo Indian peoples were living there. Arkansas was carved out of the Louisiana Purchase territory, a vast area of land that the United States had bought from France in 1803. Settlers of Irish, Scottish, and English origin soon began arriving. Arkansas became a state on June 15, 1836.

The approach of the Civil War found Arkansas divided into antislavery and proslavery groups. At first the state chose to remain in the Union, but in May 1861 it voted to secede. Long after the war, state authorities were still withholding the civil rights of black people. During the 1950s, however, the issue of black students' being allowed to enter Little Rock's Central High School made the headlines. It marked the beginning of the struggle for public-school desegregation throughout the nation.

18

**Question**: Where can you find the only diamond mine in North America?

**Answer**: At Crater of Diamonds State Park near Murfreesboro, Arkansas. Visitors are allowed to search the open fields for diamonds and may keep any they find, provided the diamond weighs no more than five carats!

# James Black and the "Arkansas Toothpick"

Ask most people what an "Arkansas toothpick" is and they'll probably shake their heads and give you a puzzled look. But folks who've been around Arkansas for a while will tell you right off that old-time Arkansans are sometimes called "toothpicks."

Does this mean that all people from Arkansas are supposed to be tall and skinny? No, it doesn't. In fact, an Arkansas toothpick isn't an ordinary toothpick at all. It's actually a very special kind of hunting knife.

The hunting knife was one of the earliest tools developed by humans. The first knives were fashioned out of sharpened stone or volcanic glass, because metal-working was unknown. Yet, these primitive knives could do all sorts of useful things. By the time the American frontier was being explored, every scout and settler owned some kind of steel-bladed knife that was keen enough to skin a deer, slit a fish, or cut up a chunk of bear meat. And, in Arkansas, if a shred of tough bear steak got caught between your teeth, there was nothing wrong with removing it—carefully, of course—with the tip of your Arkansas toothpick.

What was it, though, that made Arkansas knives so special? The answer goes back to the year 1824 when a young man by the name of James Black arrived in the village of Washington, in southwestern Arkansas Territory. Black had been born in New Jersey in 1800. At the age of eight he'd run away from home to escape his harsh stepmother. Like so many other fugitive children of that time, he soon found himself working as an apprentice. After many years of learning to be a silversmith in Philadelphia, James Black made his way west until he reached Washington, Arkansas.

There wasn't much call for the craft of silver-plating on the Arkansas frontier. But Black received a job offer from a blacksmith named Shaw. While Shaw

and his two sons were skilled at repairing farming equipment and shoeing horses, they needed somebody who had a finer touch for the making of knives and guns.

Before long, James Black's skill at turning out exceptional knives became known well beyond the Territory of Arkansas. All through the South and the Southwest, people began to tell tales of Black's "hickory test," which only *his* knives could pass.

The hickory test worked like this. A newly-made knife was used to whittle away at a stick of very hard hickory wood for one hour. After that, it still had to be sharp enough to shave the hair from a man's arm without nicking the skin. If one of James Black's knives failed to pass the test, he threw it away.

When Jim Bowie, a colorful adventurer and hot-tempered fighter of the frontier, heard about James Black's knives, he vowed that he would have one. Born in 1799, Bowie, while still in his teens, had become widely known as a daredevil who rode alligators and roped wild horses and cattle. Later, he became a lumberman, a land speculator, and a gold prospector. After a violent hand-to-hand fight in which Bowie received a cut from his own blade, he made his way to Washington, Arkansas, to have James Black make him a knife. It was

to have a horn handle, a two-edged blade, and a wide metal guard between the handle and the blade. Black followed Bowie's design fairly closely. But he tempered the steel by his secret process until it was razor sharp, and he added a few extra design features of his own.

Jim Bowie returned several weeks later to pick up the finished knife, declaring it to be the finest he'd ever owned. Soon, everybody was referring to this new model as the "Bowie knife." Orders began pouring in to James Black for a knife "just like Bowie's." Only Black knew how to produce the knife: its fine design, the balance that made it easy to throw, the extra fine quality of the steel.

Sadly, both James Black and Jim Bowie were to have lives with tragic endings, one dying young and the other living into a disabling old age. Jim Bowie's life ended in Texas in 1836, defending the Alamo against the Mexicans. It is said that he still possessed the original Bowie knife that James Black had made for him, and that it was burned along with his body at the site of the Texans' defeat.

Black's early years in Arkansas were happy enough. Soon after he had started to work for the blacksmith, Shaw, he had fallen deeply in love with Shaw's daughter, Anne. Shaw, for some reason of his own, was violently opposed to the match. But James Black and Anne Shaw married anyway.

At first, everything went extremely well for the young couple. Starting around 1830, Black's success with the Bowie knife put him into business for himself, and he and Anne had four children, three boys and a girl.

Then, in 1836—the same year that Bowie was killed—Anne died, striking the first severe blow in James Black's life. To make matters worse, her death seemed to increase Shaw's fury against Black. Perhaps he felt that frequent childbearing in his daughter's marriage to Black had ruined her health. Perhaps he was jealous of Black's skills and the fame he had achieved.

In any case, one day in 1839 the crazed Shaw visited his son-in-law who lay in bed suffering with a fever. Inflamed with anger and grief, Shaw brushed past his grandchildren, who were tending their sick father, and began beating his helpless victim viciously with a club. Black would surely have been killed if not for his dog. The animal sprang at Shaw, seized him by the throat, and drove him away.

James Black, though, was never to be the same. The beating had injured his eyes and left him half-blind. For a few more years he plied his trade. But soon he began to lose his sight completely. Gradually, too, his mind began to fade.

James Black had fully intended to pass on the secret of his forging process to his sons and to a young helper named Daniel Webster Jones, who was one of the few people admitted to the curtained-off section at the rear of Black's shop. After Black could no longer work, he lived for many years in the home of young Jones, who later became governor of the state of Arkansas.

Shortly before his death in 1872, Black made a determined effort to recall the details of his forging process so that Governor Jones could write it down to be taken up with pride by other Arkansans in the blacksmith trade. Black remembered that there had been ten or twelve processes through which he put his blades to temper the steel. But the moments of clear focus in his memory were too fleeting. Try as he might, he could not relate the sequence of the steps, or what they had consisted of.

The effort, in fact, was such a strain that the sightless Black collapsed in tears and despair. Never again, in the months remaining to him, did even a glimmer of his secret return. On June 22, 1872, it died with him.

Many so-called Bowie knives were manufactured after Black had ceased to make them. But it was said that none were ever of the quality of the knife that Bowie had helped to design and Black had produced. Although Black had tragically forgotten what had once been his greatest skill, Arkansas has not forgotten James Black.

Today we can visit the tiny but historic Arkansas town of Washington, once a crossroads for travelers en route from Missouri to Texas and the site of the tavern where the Texas Revolution was planned. There, in Old Washington Historic State Park, is a replica of the shop in which James Black turned out the first authentic Bowie knife, affectionately known to this day as the Arkansas toothpick.

# CALIFORNIA

CAPITAL: SACRAMENTO

No one is sure how California got its name. Some think it came from the first Spanish visitors of the 1500s, whose imagination had been fired by a romantic adventure tale that was published in Spain in 1510. The story described a fabulous island of great wealth and beauty called California. Even though the real California was not an island—and gold would not be discovered there for hundreds of years—the name seemed just right for it. The nickname, *The Golden State*, however, is said to derive from the rich golden-brown color of California's hills rather than from any early sign of treasure.

The third largest state, after Alaska and Texas, California has the highest waterfall in North America, Yosemite Falls (2,425 feet), and the lowest land point in the Western Hemisphere, Death Valley (282

MISSION SAN CARLOS BORROMEO AT CARMEL FOUNDED 1770

feet below sea level). It also has what are believed to be the world's oldest, largest, and tallest living trees.

More than a hundred thousand Indians of many different groups were living in California when the Spanish came north from Mexico and began to colonize them. Settlers from eastern states started to arrive in the early 1800s. But it was independence from Mexico *and* the discovery of gold, in 1848, that quickly led to statehood, on September 9, 1850. Today California has more people than any other state. They range from migrant farm workers to Hollywood superstars. California leads both in agriculture and in the aerospace and electronic industries, and is a highly varied vacationland.

---

**Question**: Where has the highest temperature in the Western Hemisphere been recorded?

**Answer**: In California's Death Valley. It was 134 degrees Fahrenheit in the shade at five feet above ground level. At ground level, the temperature has been known to reach 201 degrees Fahrenheit.

---

# The Forty-niners in Death Valley

To take the shortcut or not? That was the question that faced the members of the wagon train as they sat around the campfire on the night of November 3, 1849. All were headed for the newly discovered California gold country. Some were men on their own. But many of the travelers were entire families, hoping to make a better life in that land of newfound riches. Their ox-drawn wagons, known as prairie schooners, were laden with all their worldly goods and as much food as they could carry for the journey.

Some of the families were from as far east as Illinois and had been on the trail since April. Now they were in the barren borderlands of the future states of Nevada and California. Their leader, Captain Jefferson Hunt, gravely announced that the best route from here to the Sacramento gold region was by way of the Spanish Trail. True, it was roundabout, looping far to the south before turning north. True, it would mean another nine weeks of traveling for the weary, impatient "forty-niners." But the Spanish Trail was a route that offered fresh water and game, a slow but reliable route.

A few members of the party shook their heads doubtfully. What about a more direct route, one that headed due west? All they had was a crude map. It had been hand drawn, following the markings that an Indian chief had made in the sand with a stick. But taking the shortcut meant they'd be in the gold country in two weeks instead of nine.

Captain Hunt gave those who disagreed with him a grim stare. He was a silent, demanding man, and as the paid leader of the wagon train, he didn't like being crossed. "All I have to say," the captain remarked stonily, "is that if you take that route you will all be landed in Hell."

Next day, despite Captain Hunt's warning, a group of twenty-seven split off from the wagon train to attempt the shortcut. Entering through a mountain pass from the east, they soon found themselves in a great valley hemmed in by mountains as far as they could see. Down, down they went into the furnacelike basin. In places the valley floor was bare earth or sand; in others it was made up of gravel or large rocks. Elsewhere in the valley were glittering salt flats. The sun blazed, only a thin scattering of desert shrubs were to be seen, and the few streams or pools of water were salty and bad tasting.

Arguments soon arose about the best way to escape the valley. Several wagons turned off to try their luck in a southerly direction, and only two families remained. They were those of Asa Bennett and J. B. Arcane, accompanied by two young men who had joined up with them. One was William Lewis Manly. He had become friendly with Asa Bennett and his family back in Salt Lake City. The other young man was John Rogers, from the mountains of Tennessee.

The two families realized that they were in danger of not getting out of the valley alive. They had heard that a group of Shoshoni Indians made their home in the valley, surviving on roots, pine nuts, mesquite beans, insects, lizards, and wood rats. Yet as one member of the party later wrote, "We had seen no living creature in this desert." It was possible that the Indians had watched the wagons creak slowly onward. But they kept out of sight because their own rations were too limited to share.

Soon the dry bread that the Bennetts and the Arcanes had saved for their children gave out, and they were forced to start killing and eating their oxen. Reaching a rare spring of fresh water, the group decided to camp while the two young men, Manly and Rogers, went on foot to try to find a way through the snow-capped mountains to the west. Perhaps, with luck, they'd be back within ten days.

Driven by the thought of the women and children huddled in the shade beneath the wagons, the two men pressed on. Soon their canteens were empty and they were chewing on the stems of desert plants for moisture. They became maddened with thirst and could not swallow the ox meat they carried.

Unable to sleep, they set out very early one morning and came upon a thin sheet of ice that had formed in a canyon bottom during the chilly desert night. Quickly they broke and ate the ice, managing to chew and swallow some of the ox meat as well. Finding the ice was a great stroke of luck, for it made their survival possible. An hour or so later the sun would have risen, melting the ice and evaporating the water. The bodies of Manly and Rogers would almost certainly have been added to those of others they had passed, travelers who'd died seeking a way out of the valley. The scouting mission took Manly and Rogers twenty-six days instead of ten, as had been hoped. But they did manage to cross the mountains and reach a Mexican settlement, where they were given supplies for the return trip—food, water, horses, and a little blind mule that plodded on after the horses had to be left behind. At last the anxious moment arrived when Manly and Rogers came in sight of the wagons of the Bennetts and the Arcanes.

Everything appeared so quiet in the little encampment. Were the stranded men, women, and children still alive?

Manly fired a shot of greeting. "Then," as he later wrote, ". . . a man came out from under a wagon . . . threw his arms up high over his head and shouted, 'The boys have come! The boys have come!' "

After tears, embraces, and tales of their near-death adventure, Manly and Rogers prepared to lead the Bennetts and the Arcanes out of the valley. The families' wagons, with their furniture and other household contents, would have to be left behind, for there was no way the wagons could be hauled up the mountains or navigate the narrow cliff-side trails. So most of the party climbed out of the valley on foot, while the weaker members and a few supplies were carried on the backs of the remaining oxen.

Once the Bennetts and the Arcanes reached the snowy heights, they stopped to glance back down at the seething valley floor that had nearly taken their lives. The Indians were known to call the area "ground afire." But it was Mrs. Bennett who gave it the name by which it would be known to all future travelers. With a parting glance, she murmured, "Good-bye, death valley."

Her words were recalled by William Lewis Manly, who many years later, in 1894, published his famous account of the hardships and terrors that he, Rogers, and the other forty-niners had encountered. He called his story of courage and survival *Death Valley in '49.*

# COLORADO

CAPITAL: DENVER

*C*olorado is Spanish for "colored red." Spanish visitors of the 1500s gave this name to the Colorado River because it flows through gorges of reddish stone. Much of the state of Colorado lies in the Rocky Mountains, making it the nation's highest state on average. It has more than a thousand peaks that are over ten thousand feet high. And more than fifty of these soar to over fourteen thousand feet.

The spine of the Rockies, which zigzags through Colorado from north to south, forms part of the Continental Divide. West of the Divide, all waters flow toward the Pacific Ocean; east of the Divide, they drain toward the Atlantic.

CLIFF DWELLING

Cliff-dwelling Indians lived in the Colorado region until the 1200s, when severe drought led to crop failures and drove them from their homes. In the 1600s and 1700s, both Spain and France laid claim to the area. Some of the present-day state of Colorado came to the United States through the Louisiana Purchase of 1803, and some was ceded after the Mexican War, in 1848. A gold strike in 1858 brought a rush of easterners, and the discovery of silver lodes in 1864 led to the nickname *The Silver State.*

Colorado is also nicknamed *The Centennial State* because it joined the Union in 1876, the year of the hundredth anniversary of the signing of the Declaration of Independence. The exact date of admission was August 1. Although many early Colorado mining communities are now ghost towns, the state's mineral resources are still an important part of its economy.

---

**Question**: There is only one place in the United States where four states meet. Where is it?

**Answer**: At the southwestern corner of Colorado. The borders of Colorado, Utah, Arizona, and New Mexico join at a spot marked by the Four Corners Monument.

---

# Silver King of the Rockies

Horace Tabor had a dream, a dream of one day becoming a millionaire. So it wasn't surprising that, like thousands of other Americans of the mid-1800s, he carefully followed the news of gold strikes in the American West.

Tabor had been born in Vermont in 1830 and had worked there as a stonecutter. The future looked bleak, so he moved on to Kansas, where he tried farming. Then, in 1858, he heard about the discovery of gold nuggets in the hills west of Denver, Colorado. Soon he was part of the gold rush of 1859, remembered for the slogan "Pikes Peak or bust!"

Pikes Peak lay south of Denver, and it wasn't really where the gold had been found. But the 14,110-foot mountain was the best-known landmark in the Colorado region at the time. It had been mapped by Zebulon Pike, an American army officer, back in 1806.

Horace Tabor decided that a gold-mining strip called California Gulch, in the Colorado mining settlement of Oro City, seemed promising. He tried both mining and storekeeping there. One of the main problems the miners had was separating the gold from the heavy black sand in which it was found. So Tabor began grubstaking—contributing money to other miners for a share of the profits—rather than doing the work himself. If the gold "panned out," he made a little money. If not, he lost his investment.

The Oro City mine was profitable until about 1870. The word *oro* is Spanish for "gold," but by then strikes were becoming scarce, and Oro City itself seemed well on its way to becoming just another ghost town.

Still, some residents hung on, and Horace Tabor was one of them. Then, in 1878, after waiting patiently for nearly eighteen years, he struck—silver! Two miners, to whom Tabor had given seventeen dollars as a grubstake for a third of the profits, found that the reason the black sand near Oro City was so heavy was that it contained lead. Mingled with the lead was a tremendously rich lode of silver.

Tabor's share of the silver find gave him enough money to buy up claims all over the district, including one that turned out to be the famous Matchless Mine. The Matchless alone was soon yielding enough silver to bring in a hundred thousand dollars a month. A new town named Leadville was built near the old gold-mining site of Oro City. Its population soared to thirty thousand. By 1879, Leadville had four banks, four churches, ten dry-goods stores, over thirty restaurants, and more than a hundred saloons and gambling houses. And Horace Tabor was its mayor and postmaster.

Horace Tabor's dream had come true. As "the Silver King of the Rockies," he was now worth nine million dollars. He wanted to give something back to Leadville, so he built a four-story brick opera house, furnished with flowered carpets, red plush seats, and painted and gilded ceilings. The Tabor Grand Opera House in Leadville opened on November 30, 1879. Like most "opera houses" of the old West, it presented a wide variety of entertainment—acrobats and trained-animal acts, minstrel shows and lectures, performances of Shakespeare's plays and Harriet Beecher Stowe's *Uncle Tom's Cabin,* as well as some operas and ballets.

The audiences boasted gentlemen in black silk top hats and ladies in richly beaded gowns. They also included rough miners in heavy boots. And it wasn't unusual to pass the hanged bodies of horse thieves and murderers in the courthouse square as one entered the Tabor Grand for an evening of music or theater.

Horace Tabor's personal life changed too as he became a lavish spender. He divorced his wife of many years, Augusta, and was secretly married in 1882 to Elizabeth Doe, a divorced miner's wife with whom he had fallen wildly in love. "Baby" Doe, as she was called, was thirty years younger than Horace, who was then fifty-two. Some people in Leadville felt the whole affair was scandalous and that Horace had made a fool of himself.

But he and the beautiful Baby Doe went on to enjoy the pleasures of both money and public life. Horace served as lieutenant governor of Colorado and even filled out a vacated term as a United States senator in 1883. While he and Baby Doe were in Washington, they were remarried in a public ceremony at the elegant Willard Hotel, with President Chester A. Arthur as guest of honor.

Throughout the 1880s it seemed like the Silver King of the Rockies had it all, that his bubble of happiness would never burst. Then, in 1893, a financial panic hit the United States. The government, which had been buying silver to benefit the western states, repealed the Sherman Silver Purchase Act, and the entire Colorado silver market collapsed. Almost overnight Horace Tabor found himself a ruined man, his vast fortune gone.

Now, the citizens back in Leadville muttered among themselves, now we'll see how long Baby Doe will stay with Horace Tabor. They waited. Horace became ill, a broken man. But Baby Doe remained at his side, trying to nurse him back to health. Still Horace's life ebbed slowly away. On his deathbed in 1899, his last words to Baby Doe were, "Hang on to the Matchless." He had never stopped believing that the value of silver would come back, and that the Matchless Mine up in the hills outside Leadville would once again make millions.

Baby Doe followed Horace's instructions faithfully. Living in extreme poverty, ignored by everyone, she remained for thirty-six years in a cabin near the mine. In the winter of 1935 she was found there, frozen to death. She had lived to be seventy-five, her youth and beauty long gone. But her love and loyalty had proved to be everlasting. So touching was the story of Baby Doe that in 1955 the American composer Douglas Moore wrote an opera about her and Horace Tabor called *The Ballad of Baby Doe*. Based on true events, and with words by John LaTouche, the opera's gala first performance was given in Colorado—the state that had inspired it—at the Central City Opera House, on July 7, 1956.

TABOR AFTER GOING BROKE

# CONNECTICUT

The Mohican Indians, members of the Algonquian family, used the term *Quinnehtukqet*, "beside the long tidal river," to describe the area where they lived. In time this word became Connecticut. It applied to the southward-flowing Connecticut River, which is the longest in New England, to the colony, and later to the state.

Puritans from the Massachusetts Bay Colony who were dissatisfied with their government resettled in the Connecticut region in the 1630s. Soon they formed their own government and were prospering as farmers, artisans, and seafarers. During the American Revolution, George Washington praised the Connecticut colony for cannons given to the Continental Army.

One of Connecticut's nicknames is *The Constitution State*, because its colonial laws served, in part, as a model for the United States Constitution. Connecticut became the fifth state of the new nation on January 9, 1788. During the 1800s, farming gradually gave way to the manufacturing of clocks and watches, metalware, firearms, and textiles. Today Connecticut produces submarines, aircraft engines, and helicopters. The state also has sandy beaches and gentle, rolling countryside, and strongly appeals to visitors because of its richly preserved colonial past.

PURITANS

35

**Question**: The term "Connecticut Yankee" has long been used to describe someone who lives in that state. Where does the word "Yankee" come from?

**Answer**: Most people think it comes from a Dutch name, Jan Kees. This was the Dutch equivalent of "John Doe," a name used on a legal paper when a person's real name is unknown.

# Don't Take Any Wooden Nutmegs

No sooner had the colony of Connecticut started to fill up with settlers than the Yankee peddler was born. A Yankee peddler was just that—a native of New England who set out with a pack on his back, or with a horse and wagon, to sell all kinds of necessities to farmers and villagers who lived some distance from coastal towns and cities.

At first, little more than Indian foot trails took the peddlers to the inland settlements. Sometimes a river or a large lake served as a "road" to the peddler's customers. He would load his stock into a canoe or onto a flatboat. Then he'd land at waterside communities with "a whole raft of goods."

By the 1700s almost everyone who lived on an isolated farm or in a village too small to have a general store depended on the yearly or seasonal visit of the Yankee peddler who, more often than not, came from Connecticut. And as roads were carved out of the wilderness, peddlers began to travel much greater distances from home, going as far west as Ohio and Kentucky and reaching south into the Carolinas and Georgia.

What did people buy from the Yankee peddler? Just about anything they couldn't hunt, grow, or make for themselves. They bought needles and pins, scissors, straight razors for shaving, paper for writing, tinware and pewter for cooking and serving food. They bought mirrors, small pieces of glass to use as window panes, guns and gunpowder for hunting, axes for felling trees, and planting and cutting tools for farming.

A visit from a Yankee peddler was usually eagerly awaited. He brought news and gossip of the outside world. His pack or wagon also contained luxury items that today we would consider necessities, such as clocks or eyeglasses. Frontier settlers were dazzled by the ribbons and laces the peddler sold and by the lengths of factory-made, brightly colored cloth that were so much prettier than the drab homespun from their own looms. Brass buttons and brass combs were also greatly favored over the crude homemade kind of bone or wood. And where else could you buy coffee, tea, sugar, and salt, and spices for preserving and flavoring, such as pepper, cloves, ginger, and nutmeg?

Up to the time of the American Revolution, almost everything the Yankee peddler sold was imported. Manufactured items of metal, glass, and cloth came mainly from England, which had strict laws forbidding the colonies from having factories or even small workshops that might compete with those of the mother country. Coffee came from Arabia, tea from India, sugar from the West Indies, and spices from the far-off East Indies.

The life of a colonial traveling salesman wasn't an easy one. Roads were either muddy or dusty. Roadside inns were few and far between, with lumpy beds and badly cooked food. And payment for the peddler's wares often came in the form of deerskins, beaver pelts, or farm products rather than money. Most peddlers were honest. But they were all out to clear as much profit as they could from a long, uncomfortable jaunt on the road. And this led to complaints, here and there, from their customers.

Rumors started cropping up about a peddler who'd sold a clock that stopped running as soon as he'd rounded the bend in the road, or a barometer that never showed a change in the weather. To some people a Yankee peddler was a sharp trader, a person who would cheat you if you didn't watch out. He might sell you a cigar or even a whole ham that looked exactly like the real thing but turned out to be made of wood. The most likely item in a crooked peddler's pack, especially if he came from Connecticut, was said to be a wooden nutmeg.

A wooden nutmeg looked just like a *real* nutmeg kernel, the kind you grated into a powdery spice to put into a pudding or a pie. But when you rubbed it along the side of the grater, it turned out to be a nugget of wood, colored and even scented to resemble the nutmegs that were grown in the Spice Islands of distant Indonesia. Southerners got especially mad at Yankee peddlers whom they suspected of being dishonest. The term "damn Yankee" was coined long before the Civil War. As to the wooden nutmeg story, it led to

NUTMEGS: 1¢

a second nickname for *The Constitution State*: *The Nutmeg State*. And ever since, another name for people from Connecticut has been Nutmeggers.

Actually, it's highly doubtful that anybody would have gone to the trouble of carving an imitation nutmeg. Cargoes of real nutmegs arrived quite regularly at New England ports, and they sold for only about a penny apiece. The warning "Don't take any wooden nutmegs" may even have been started by the owners of the general stores that were opening up in many villages and crossroad communities. The retailers were afraid of being undersold by the peddlers and didn't want any of them roaming about in their part of the countryside.

Around 1860, when coins made of nickel began to be minted in the United States, a new popular expression arose. "Don't take any wooden nickels," the wary citizens cautioned one another, even though some of the early nickels were worth as little as three cents.

By the mid-1800s, in any case, the day of the long-distance peddler was pretty well over. Many of the Yankee peddlers decided to give up their traveling lives, settle down in one place, and become the proprietors of general stores themselves.

rooster, endowed with the physical strength, speed, and courage of a winning gamecock. When their regiment finally met the British, nothing was going to hold it back.

It seemed, though, that British troops were *never* going to march into colonial Delaware, no matter how eager for battle the Blue Hen's Chickens were. Then, at last, on September 3, 1777—nearly two and a half years after the war had begun—an advance unit of the British Army turned up at a village called Cooch's Bridge, just south of the town of Newark, Delaware. The Blue Hens were ready for them.

Maybe the Battle of Cooch's Bridge was a mere skirmish compared to the really big battles of the American Revolution. But the

fighters of the Delaware regiment made such a name for themselves that they went on to fight outside the colony. One of them, Captain Robert Kirkwood, was said to have risked his life thirty-three times for his country before he lost it in action, truly a Blue Hen fighter to the death.

As for the British who first sampled the fury of Delaware's colonial militia, they made no further efforts to penetrate Delaware itself. In fact, they quickly moved on into Pennsylvania.

One of the stories connected with the Battle of Cooch's Bridge is that it was the first at which the thirteen-star American flag was flown throughout the fray. The Continental Congress had approved the design of the flag just months earlier, on June 14, 1777.

Today cockfighting is illegal in the United States. But the bravery of those who named themselves the Blue Hen's Chickens lives on. Since that famous day at Cooch's Bridge in 1777, all Delawareans have been known as Blue Hens. And after statehood was achieved in 1787, one of Delaware's nicknames became *The Blue Hen State.*

# DISTRICT OF COLUMBIA

The nation's capital is a city that is not located in any state. Its present-day area was carved out of the state of Maryland. Between 1791 and 1846, Washington, D.C., also included parts of the Virginia locales of Alexandria and Arlington. "D.C." stands for District of Columbia. The word "Columbia" is derived from Christopher Columbus. "Washington" comes directly from George Washington. But the first president never actually served there. The city was still being planned and built during George Washington's two terms in office, from 1789 to 1797.

Even John Adams, the second president, lived in Washington only from 1800 to 1801, his last year in office, because its buildings weren't ready for occupancy. The nation's capital was laid out by the French engineer Pierre L'Enfant as a city of spacious circles, with broad avenues radiating from them like the spokes of a wheel.

Well into the 1800s, though, Washington's development was slow. Part of the land on which it was to be built was a mosquito-infested swamp. For years after the city had become the nation's capital, its streets were muddy, farm animals roamed freely on the grounds of the President's House, and hunting parties shot quail within sight of the still-unfinished Capitol building. Progress was further

PIERRE L'ENFANT

slowed when, during the War of 1812, the British burned the President's House, the Capitol, and other public buildings.

---

**Question**: How did the White House get its name?
**Answer**: Following the War of 1812, the walls of the blackened stone mansion where the president lived were restored by being painted a blinding white. From then on, the building was referred to as the White House, a name that finally became official in 1902.

---

# Dolley Madison Stands Her Ground

"Dear Sister," Dolley Madison wrote hastily from the President's House in Washington on an August day in 1814, "I [am] ready at a moment's warning to enter my carriage and leave the city."

Through that day and part of the next, Dolley added several more anxious paragraphs. Finally, she closed her letter with the lines, "When I shall again write to you, or where I shall be tomorrow, I cannot tell!"

How different everything was on this stifling summer afternoon than it was a little over five years ago, when Dolley and her husband James Madison had danced at their first inaugural ball. Proudly, the newly-elected fourth president of the United States and his young wife had greeted all those in attendance. Madison was a short man, even a "withered little apple-John," according to the writer Washington Irving. But Dolley, as she always had, looked like a queen. She was dressed in a gown of rich yellow velvet and wore a headdress of satin trimmed with long, elegant feathers.

Today, though, the city was filled with fear and dread. President Madison himself had left Washington to join up with the troops standing ready to defend it. The War of 1812 was still going on, and now the British were threatening to advance on the nation's capital and destroy it.

Some people in the government and in the country had blamed

the president for becoming
involved in yet another war with
England so soon after the
American Revolution. Bitterly,
they called it "Mr. Madison's war."

It was far too late, though, for
worrying about who was to
blame. The president's wife
knew only that she must load
what she could—private cabinet
papers, public documents, the
presidential silver and other
valuable items—into the waiting
wagon. Already two messengers
and a trusted family friend had
arrived, urging her to flee, for
a battle was taking place at
Bladensburg, Maryland, on the
city's outskirts.

But Dolley still held back.
There was something that she
must take with her, something
large and heavy and securely
fastened to the wall of the
President's House. It was a
famous portrait of George
Washington that had been
painted by the artist Gilbert
Stuart in 1793. How could she
possibly leave this behind for
the British to slash or burn?

Arguments followed, as the
dust-covered messengers stood
panting nearby, as the friend
come to hasten Dolley's
departure pleaded with her. The
servants awaited their orders.
Already they had helped Dolley

DRESSED AS A FARMER'S WIFE

dress herself as a farmer's wife rather than a first lady, to disguise her in the event they were captured by the enemy. There was no more time to lose.

At last Dolley reached a decision, painful though it was. She knew that the entire portrait could not possibly be taken down from the wall in the few moments remaining. Instead, she ordered that the canvas be cut away from its frame so that it could be rolled up and hidden for safekeeping. Quickly, Dolley's instructions were carried out. It was done! Now she could make her escape.

That evening the British forces did indeed enter the city, and one detachment made straight for the President's House. There the soldiers found the dinner table set for forty guests, joints of roasted meat in the kitchen, and crystal decanters of wine on the sideboard. Dolley Madison was a renowned Washington hostess and, even in the midst of an invasion, she had been planning one of her dinner parties.

Delighted, the British sat down to this unexpected treat, drank freely of the wine, and ended their feast by setting fire to the house. All night the city blazed, as public buildings, ships, and munitions storehouses spluttered and exploded. Only a late-night thunderstorm prevented the flames from totally destroying the President's House.

When the tide of war finally turned and the Madisons were able to return to Washington, they found that their former home was little more than a blackened shell. It would have to be almost completely rebuilt and its stone walls painted white to hide the fire damage.

President and Mrs. Madison had to live out the three remaining years of his second term in temporary Washington quarters. "Queen Dolley," however, kept her good humor and her gracious ways. She had never denied her love of luxury and stylish entertaining. But in the emergency of war, she had risked her own welfare to save a precious symbol of the nation's heritage. The portrait of George Washington that Dolley saved can be seen today hanging in the East Room of the White House.

# FLORIDA

The first European to see Florida was the conquistador Juan Ponce de León, on Easter Sunday in the year 1513. He found the coast covered with colorful blooms and named it *Pascua florida*, the Spanish words for "flowery Easter." Florida's nicknames include *The Peninsula State*, because of the way it juts into the sea to form the southeastern tip of the continental United States. Another nickname, *The Sunshine State*, refers to Florida's mostly warm and sunny weather, which means rich vegetation and animal life—and, of course, vacationers galore.

TOURISTS

Indians in large numbers had been living in Florida for thousands of years before the Spanish, French, and British began to struggle for its possession. They included Timucuan and Apalachee peoples in the north, Calusa and Tegesta groups in the south. The United States received Florida from Spain in 1821. But bitter and bloody wars with the Seminole Indians continued until 1842, when most of the defeated Indians were banished from their Florida lands to the Oklahoma territory. Florida became a state on March 3, 1845.

**Question**: What is the oldest permanent European settlement in the United States?

**Answer**: St. Augustine, Florida. It was near this site that Juan Ponce de León landed in 1513 to begin his search for the legendary Fountain of Youth. But St. Augustine itself was founded in 1565 by another Spanish navigator, Pedro Menéndez de Avilés.

# The Oranges of Lue Gim Gong

Very early on a cool, misty morning in the year 1886, Lue Gim Gong did a terrible thing. He stole away from his village home in southern China, leaving behind the bride he was to marry that very day. Lue knew that his mother would be brokenhearted, that his entire family would be disgraced, that he would never again be able to return to China.

Yet Lue could not face the life that lay ahead of him in the tiny Chinese village of Lung On. Although he was only in his mid-twenties, he had already had a very strange adventure. At the age of thirteen Lue had been transported, along with about fifty other teenage boys from China, to San Francisco and then across America to the town of North Adams, Massachusetts, to work for three years in a shoe factory.

Chinese immigrants had started coming to California during the gold rush of 1849. By the time Lue arrived, around 1870, there were a great many Chinese in the American West, working mainly as cooks and servants, and farm and railroad laborers. But on the East Coast, where Lue was put to work, there were probably fewer than a hundred Chinese.

Lue's job at the shoe factory was hard and the hours were long. The lives of the Chinese were threatened by union workers who had lost their jobs to the lower-paid Chinese youths. Strikers sometimes threw stones at the Chinese. The building in which they lived, just behind the factory, was little better than a prison.

Yet Lue had come to prefer his life in America. And when the three years were up he did not want to return to China. The main reason was his teacher, Miss Fanny Burlingame. Along with the other Chinese factory boys, Lue had been attending a Sunday school run by the Methodists and Baptists of the town. There he had learned English. He had also studied mathematics and religion. Soon he was taking extra lessons in high-school-level subjects with Miss Fanny, including botany. Miss Fanny's family had a greenhouse in which she and her father experimented with growing new flower and plant varieties. This greatly interested Lue, for as a child he had helped his mother at work in the orange groves of his home village. One of the things she had shown him was how to improve the fruit by joining the wood of different trees, in a process known as grafting.

In order to be near Miss Fanny, Lue decided to continue working at the shoe factory in North Adams. He was baptized a Christian and became a member of the First Baptist Church, like the Burlingame family. He cut off the long pigtail that many Chinese of his day wore, and he dressed in Western clothing.

Life would have been almost perfect except that Lue's health began to fail. His body had suffered for years from a poor diet and harsh living and working conditions. In 1886 he was told that he had tuberculosis and might not survive another winter in Massachusetts. It was then that he returned to the warmer climate of southern China, only to find that he could no longer be part of the old ways of his village.

When Lue returned to America, he learned that Miss Fanny—who herself suffered from a lung problem—was wintering in De Land, Florida, where her sister and brother-in-law owned five acres of orange groves. They needed a manager for the groves and also someone to help out around the house. Cut off forever from his own family, Lue agreed to work for Miss Fanny's relatives. Miss Fanny looked on Lue as an adopted son, and Lue even thought of her as "Mother Fanny." Yet, he knew that in the eyes of others he was still an "inferior" Chinese, and that some of his duties would be those of a servant.

In the years that followed, Miss Fanny and her sister bought more property in De Land, and Lue put whatever time he could into experimenting with new citrus varieties. Then, in 1903, came the real test for Lue. Mother Fanny died. Although the Florida groves owned by Miss Fanny and her sister passed to Lue, he now felt totally alone. It was almost a blessing when a severe freeze hit the groves, threatening the entire orange crop. For now Lue could forget his loneliness by burying himself in his work.

By 1909 Lue had developed a large, juicy orange that could resist the sudden cold snaps that occasionally hit central Florida. This was exactly what the Florida growers needed in order to compete successfully with the California citrus industry. Lue won a silver medal from the national fruit-growers society for his "year-round" orange, and he went on to develop hardier and better-tasting grapefruits, tangerines, mandarins, and lemons. Each crate of fruit shipped from his groves bore a label with Lue's personal guarantee of quality and of honesty and fairness in doing business, the same philosophy by which he lived.

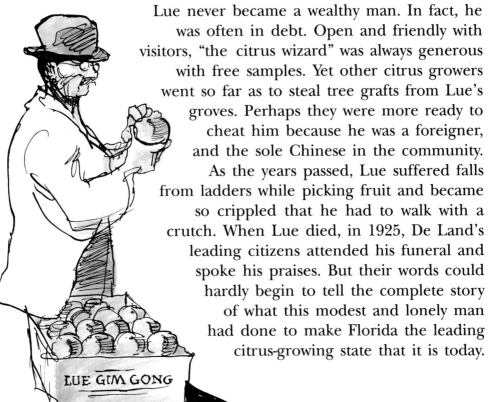

LUE GIM GONG

Lue never became a wealthy man. In fact, he was often in debt. Open and friendly with visitors, "the citrus wizard" was always generous with free samples. Yet other citrus growers went so far as to steal tree grafts from Lue's groves. Perhaps they were more ready to cheat him because he was a foreigner, and the sole Chinese in the community.

As the years passed, Lue suffered falls from ladders while picking fruit and became so crippled that he had to walk with a crutch. When Lue died, in 1925, De Land's leading citizens attended his funeral and spoke his praises. But their words could hardly begin to tell the complete story of what this modest and lonely man had done to make Florida the leading citrus-growing state that it is today.

# GEORGIA

Georgia, a onetime colony of England, was named for King George II. Among its nicknames are *The Peach State* and *The Goober State*. Georgia peaches are famous. Goobers are peanuts. "Goober" comes from the African Bantu-language word for peanut, *nguba*.

Spanish explorers reached Georgia in the 1500s and found it inhabited by Creek Indians in the south and Cherokees in the northern highlands. James Oglethorpe, an Englishman, started a colony at Savannah, on the Georgia coast, in 1733, to keep the Spanish in nearby Florida at bay.

Georgia was the last to be settled of England's group of thirteen American colonies, which won their independence in 1783. Georgia entered the Union as the fourth state, on January 2, 1788. But it seceded, as did other southern slaveholding states, at the start of the Civil War, in 1861.

Much of Georgia's wealth was destroyed during the Civil War, when the Union Army of the North burned Atlanta and marched all the way to Savannah, living off the land. Today Atlanta is a bustling modern city of "the New South," and Georgia has become a major producer of textiles and pulpwood, as well as fruits and other food crops.

---

**Question**: Which is the biggest state east of the Mississippi River?

**Answer**: Georgia. Although it ranks only twenty-first in size among the fifty states, it has the largest land area east of the Mississippi.

---

# The Little White House at Warm Springs

A wounded Creek Indian warrior may have been among the first to bathe in the mysterious spring that came bubbling out of the ground. The water of the little pool was wonderfully warm and soothing to his torn and aching flesh. Magically, too, he found that he could float in the pool without any effort. Soon others came to the warm spring, easy to find because it lay not far from the low, pine-covered mountain to the west.

Time passed. Europeans formed settlements along the coast and then farther inland. They too heard about the magic spring and sought its healing warmth. In the late 1700s a yellow-fever epidemic swept through the port city of Savannah, Georgia. Soon survivors of the disease were traveling across the state to bathe in its waters.

By 1832 a resort hotel that could accommodate two hundred guests had been built. The waters were enclosed in a series of pools,

large and small, with private ones for ladies to bathe in. In the late 1800s the springs area became part of the newly incorporated town of Bullochville, and its rebuilt hotel and cottages, featuring tennis courts, a dancing pavilion, and the health-giving pools, began to attract large numbers of fashionable visitors.

By the 1920s, however, the crowds had dwindled, partly due to the growing popularity of the automobile. Everyone seemed to want a traveling vacation rather than a stay of several weeks in one place. It appeared that the warm springs of Bullochville, in western Georgia, were on their way to being all but forgotten. Perhaps they would have been if not for an illness that struck Franklin Delano Roosevelt, a lawyer and popular political figure from New York State.

In the summer of 1921, the thirty-nine-year-old Roosevelt, healthy, energetic, and a fine sportsman, had come down with chills and fever while vacationing at his home at Campobello Island off the coast of Maine. For two weeks he lay in severe pain and partially paralyzed before his condition was diagnosed as poliomyelitis—the much-dreaded polio.

Another name for polio was infantile paralysis, because it was generally thought that only children could get it and that it always caused some part of the body to become paralyzed. Neither was completely true. But Franklin Roosevelt's case did leave his legs paralyzed. He was unable to walk without crutches and heavy, leather-and-steel leg braces that reached from hip to ankle. As each of the seven-pound braces locked at the knee, he could not walk stairs. Often he used a wheelchair to get relief from the weight and pain of the braces and crutches.

Undaunted by his disability, Roosevelt searched for a cure, even a partial one. Warm-water therapy was recommended. But there were few heated swimming pools in the 1920s. For two winters Roosevelt tried bathing in Florida, but the ocean waters were seldom warm enough.

Then one day he was told about a run-down resort in Georgia where there were natural springs with water that always registered eighty-eight degrees Fahrenheit, winter or summer. It wasn't surprising that people had once thought the springs magic, for the average rain temperature in the area was much cooler, only sixty-two degrees Fahrenheit.

Geologists, however, had learned that the rainwater that fell on nearby Pine Mountain went into the ground to the astonishing depth of thirty-eight hundred feet. There it absorbed minerals from the rocks and was warmed by the earth. The spring waters that emerged were heated and were laden with minerals that were beneficial for pain and inflammation of the joints, muscles, and other tissues. Taken internally, the waters were also recommended for stomach, liver, and kidney problems.

In October 1924, on his way to Florida, Roosevelt stopped at the Georgia warm springs. The hotel and cottages *were* old and shabby. But the moment Roosevelt entered the pool and the warm water engulfed his legs, he declared, "How marvelous it feels. I don't think I'll ever get out!" Although his legs were extremely thin and weak, he was actually able to stand and even walk unaided in only four feet of water.

Roosevelt soon began inviting other people who had had polio to Warm Springs (which in 1924 had officially changed its name from Bullochville), and in 1926 he bought the resort from its owner and began making plans for a treatment center for patients who, like himself, had been left with permanent disabilities. The pool facilities were much improved, exercise and therapy equipment was installed, and the entire nonprofit complex became known as the Georgia Warm Springs Foundation. It would function through the 1950s, at which time the conquest of polio began.

Franklin Delano Roosevelt went on to become governor of New York State for two terms, from 1929 to 1933, and then United States president, the only one to be elected to third and fourth terms. He entered office during the worst depression the nation had ever experienced, and he saw it through World War II almost to the surrender of Germany.

During his time in office, few people were made aware of the president's disability. Television had not yet been developed, and he spoke to the nation on the radio in a series of informal and engaging "fireside chats." When he appeared in movie-theater newsreels or newspaper photographs, only his well-developed upper body was usually shown.

LITTLE WHITE HOUSE, WARM SPRINGS, GEORGIA

In 1932 Roosevelt built a "Little White House" at Warm Springs, and throughout his presidency he considered it his second home. The house itself was remarkably simple, a one-story white clapboard cottage, its rooms paneled in natural pine. It was to Georgia that the president came in the spring of 1945 for a much-needed rest. At the age of sixty-three, he was experiencing deep weariness, and a recent trip to the Soviet Union for a conference with wartime leaders had exhausted him.

Around midday on April 12, he sat in his favorite brown-leather chair in the living-dining room of the Little White House. He was putting the finishing touches on a speech he was to deliver the following day. At the same time, he was having his portrait painted in watercolor by an artist from New York. Suddenly he slumped forward as though he were looking for something. Those who were in the room ran toward him.

Unable to sit up, the president whispered, "I have a terrific pain in the back of my head." Two members of his staff carried him to his bed. Without regaining consciousness, the president died at 3:35 that afternoon, of a massive cerebral hemorrhage, in the Little White House at Warm Springs.

The life and work of Franklin Delano Roosevelt had meant many things to many people. Among them were his fellow polio sufferers with whom he had shared the benefits he'd discovered at Georgia's Warm Springs. His contribution, though, went much further. The money raised through the March of Dimes, an organization the president had founded in 1938, helped medical researchers discover the cause of polio. As a result of the vaccines that were developed in the 1950s, polio is almost unknown today.

# HAWAII

Hawaii is known as *The Aloha State. Aloha,* the Hawaiian word for "love," is also used for greetings. It can mean "hello" or "good-bye," "welcome" or "farewell." Most of all, it expresses friendship. The first Hawaiians were Polynesians from Tahiti and other Southern Pacific islands. They arrived in huge outrigger canoes with their pigs, chickens, and favorite plant foods. Between A.D. 500 and 900, they settled on several islands—now called the High Islands—of the Hawaiian chain. These eight main islands are some of the peaks of a massive undersea volcanic mountain range that stretches nearly two thousand miles across the Pacific Ocean.

On January 20, 1778, Captain James Cook, an Englishman, came upon the lush, unspoiled islands and named them the Sandwich Islands, after the Earl of Sandwich, who had backed his expedition. The Hawaiians' own name for their land is believed to have come from one of their earlier Pacific island homes, Havaiki. Although Cook was killed during a return visit to Hawaii, European traders, whalers, and missionaries soon arrived in growing numbers. By the late 1800s Western diseases had wiped out about four-fifths of the Hawaiian population. Chinese, Japanese, Filipinos, Europeans, and Americans

CAPT. JAMES COOK

62

immigrated to the islands and blended with many of the remaining pure-blooded Hawaiians. While Hawaii was still an independent kingdom, sugarcane planters and other foreign developers pushed for the United States to annex Hawaii. When this was refused, they established an independent republic, lasting from 1894 to 1898, when Hawaii was finally annexed. It became a United States Territory in 1900 and entered the Union as the fiftieth state on August 21, 1959.

---

**Question**: What's the wettest place in the United States—and possibly in the world?

**Answer**: Mt. Waialeale, on the Hawaiian island of Kauai. Rainfall there averages 460 inches, or almost *40 feet*, a year!

---

# The Farewell Song of Queen Liliuokalani

"May [this palace] house Hawaiian nobility to the end of time." With these words of the king's prime minister, the cornerstone of Iolani Palace in Honolulu had been laid. Now, on February 12, 1883, the elegant new home of Hawaiian royalty was completed and was being dedicated in a great public ceremony.

King Kalakaua was dressed in white, his shoulders draped with a cloak made entirely of golden bird feathers, the symbol of Hawaiian rulership. A king's cape of this kind took generations to make, for each of the rare tropical birds from which the feathers were taken had only two such golden plumes. The birds themselves were never killed. They were trapped with a sticky substance, their feathers gently plucked, and then released.

The ladies of the procession wore glittering gowns ordered from London and Paris. Perhaps the most astonishing was that worn by Liliuokalani (Lee-LEE-oo-oh-kah-LAH-nee), the king's sister and heir

to the throne. The gown was made entirely of gold and white brocade raised
into tiny puffs, each puff fastened
down with a miniature golden bird.

Liliuokalani, whose name meant
"salt air of heaven," was a woman of
determination and purpose, proud of
her Hawaiian heritage yet modern in
outlook. She had been born in 1838
and had been educated at an American
missionary school from the age of four.
She had a Western name, Lydia, as well
as her Hawaiian name. And at the
age of twenty-four, she had married
a New Englander who lived in Hawaii,
John Dominis.

Liliuokalani grew up at a time when
great changes were taking place in the
Hawaiian Islands. Soon after the
islands were discovered by the outside

QUEEN LILIUOKALANI

world, in the late 1700s, traders and missionaries began to arrive.
During the 1800s more and more *haoles* (white foreigners) from the
United States settled in Hawaii. They ran the schools, the churches,
and the hospitals. They engaged in shipping and other important
businesses, and they developed large sugarcane plantations and cattle ranches. Many were also active in the royal government, and
they had already begun to press the United States for Hawaii's
annexation.

After the dedication ceremonies at Iolani Palace—with its rich
throne room and imported furniture, carpets, and chandeliers—the
foreigners' criticism of King Kalakaua was sharper than ever. They
accused him of being spendthrift and corrupt. But there was another reason they wanted to see the Hawaiian king dethroned. If Hawaii were to become an American territory, there would be no tax
on sugar and other Hawaiian products shipped to the United States.

Liliuokalani was all too aware of the plots and schemes going on
behind her brother's back. On returning from a visit to England in

1887 to celebrate the fiftieth year of rule of the great Queen Victoria, she was especially horrified to learn that the controlling interests among the *haoles* had forced a new constitution on King Kalakaua. It stripped him of many of his powers and also reduced the number of offices held by local chiefs. Little by little, Liliuokalani's dream of "Hawaii for the Hawaiians" was vanishing before her eyes.

Four years later the broken King Kalakaua died, and Liliuokalani herself ascended to the throne. From the time of her youth she had admired strong, independent-minded women. Queen Victoria of England had impressed her. But her true role model was Queen Kaahumanu, the wife of King Kamehaha I, who had unified the Hawaiian Islands in 1795. For centuries Hawaiian women had been forbidden to eat certain foods such as pork, bananas, coconuts, and certain kinds of fish. Because these foods were believed to confer special powers, they were reserved solely for men. But Queen Kaahumanu had defied these taboos, or prohibitions, and freed Hawaiian women to eat whatever foods they wished.

On becoming queen in 1891, Liliuokalani knew exactly what she must do. She must halt the trend toward an American takeover by putting through a new constitution that would limit *haole* power and allow only Hawaiian citizens the right to vote.

Liliuokalani's attempt to keep Hawaii for the Hawaiians was a brave one, but it failed. In 1893, after two stormy years, a pair of powerful American figures in Hawaii brought in the United States Marines to force the queen to surrender her authority. They were John L. Stevens, the American representative to the Islands, and a lawyer named Sanford B. Dole. When the United States president, Grover Cleveland, refused to take the imperialistic step of annexing Hawaii, the leaders set up a provisional

government, followed by an independent Hawaiian republic with Dole as president.

Even more shameful treatment awaited Liliuokalani. In January 1895 she was arrested on charges of having planned a revolt and was brought to trial. She was fined five thousand dollars and given five years at hard labor. Although the sentence was never carried out, the former queen was imprisoned for nine months in a room in Iolani Palace, which had been stripped bare of all its rich furnishings. De-

nied visitors, she passed much of her time writing music, as she had done for many years. And there, in the palace that would never again enthrone Hawaiian nobility, the first verses came to her for "Aloha Oe" ("Farewell to Thee"). This sad, lilting Hawaiian song of departure has become known throughout the world.

A little over a year after her release, Liliuokalani was granted a pardon by President Dole and was even given a United States passport. Apparently she was no longer considered a threat to the new government. Liliuokalani traveled to Boston to visit the relatives of her husband, John, who had died during her brief reign, a time when she had been most in need of his support and advice. Then she traveled to Washington, D.C., to thank President Cleveland for having opposed the annexation of Hawaii. But his term in office was already drawing to a close, and it was well known that the incoming president, William McKinley, was in favor of annexation.

In 1898 Liliuokalani was back in Hawaii, living as a private citizen. She did not attend the ceremony in Honolulu, on August 12, formally annexing Hawaii to the United States and ending all hopes for a restoration of Hawaiian rule. Liliuokalani, however, felt she had told her side of the unhappy struggle in the book she had written about her life. It was called *Hawaii's Story by Hawaii's Queen* and was published in the very year of Hawaii's annexation.

By the time of Liliuokalani's death in 1917, no further claims to the throne existed. Her niece, Princess Kaiulani, who would have been her heir, had died in 1899 at the age of twenty-three. The sad, dreaming words of Liliuokalani's song seemed best to express her vanished hopes:

> *Farewell to thee, farewell to thee,*
> *Thou . . . who dwells in shaded bowers.*
> *A fond embrace ere I depart,*
> *Until we meet again.*

SILVER KALAKAUA DOLLAR

# IDAHO

CAPITAL: BOISE

The Shoshoni Indian words *ee-dah-how,* meaning "sun coming down the mountain," gave Idaho its name. *Ee-dah-how* is also another way of saying "daybreak," because in much of this Rocky Mountain state the sun's rays must cross a lofty ridge at dawn.

The Shoshoni, the Nez Perce, and other Indian groups were living in the Idaho region when Lewis and Clark passed through it in 1805, on their expedition to the Pacific Coast. They are believed to have been the first Europeans to have visited the area. The discovery of gold in 1860 brought a mining boom. Silver and other minerals were also found, giving Idaho its nicknames *Gem of the Mountains* and, later, *The Gem State.* Cattlemen, sheep herders, and farmers followed the mining folk, leading to statehood on July 3, 1890.

SHOSHONI

Hells Canyon, carved out by the Snake River, which forms much of the border between Idaho and Oregon, is the deepest in North America. It descends more than six thousand feet, deeper even than the Grand Canyon. Idaho is also a *big* potato-growing state. Its baking potatoes are famous for their fine taste and unusually large size.

**Question:** Here's an Idaho riddle. What did the Idaho potato farmer say to the visitor who asked if he would sell him a hundred pounds of potatoes?

**Answer:** "No sir, I can't do it. Wouldn't cut into a potato for anyone!"

69

# Rendezvous of the Mountain Men

"Wanted: Enterprising Young Men . . ." This was how an attention-getting advertisement in a St. Louis newspaper, the *Missouri Gazette* of February 13, 1822, began. The ad was placed by General William H. Ashley, an explorer and fur trader, who was looking for tough, adventurous fur trappers for his newly formed Rocky Mountain Fur Company.

Hunting for the skins of buffalo, deer, and bear, and the furs of mink, fox, and beaver, wasn't new, of course. The Indians had been doing it ever since they'd arrived in North America, and so had the earliest white visitors. But once the Lewis and Clark Expedition of 1804–06 opened the way through the Rockies to the Far West, trapping had started to be big business. Beaver skins were in especially high demand because of men's hat fashions in Europe and the United States. Silky-looking top hats made of the short, glossy underfur of the beaver had become the rage starting in the early 1800s.

BEAVER AND TOP-HATTED GENT

One of the first to sign up with General Ashley was Jedediah Smith, who had recently arrived in St. Louis from the East and was looking for just such a challenge in the forested mountains of the West. Smith, in fact, soon became known as "the mountain man's mountain man" because his experiences were typical of the harsh, dangerous, and often lonely life of the trapper in the wilds.

The mountain men were shaggy, bearded, and unkempt. They dressed in ill-fitting deerskins, wore caps of coonskin or some other fur, and made their shoes out of elk or buffalo hide, like the moccasins of the Indians. Throughout the fall, winter, and spring, they holed up in the rich beaver territory that would later become the states of Idaho, Utah, and Wyoming. They lived on freshly shot meat and on rations of coffee, sugar, flour, and cornmeal, which were packed onto the back of a horse or mule along with their other supplies and the pelts they collected.

Come summer, they finally emerged from their distant haunts and came together at an appointed meeting place, or rendezvous. This was where they would sell their furs, replenish their supplies, and meet with other trappers to swap stories and let off a little steam.

One of the most popular rendezvous sites for General Ashley's mountain men was Bear Lake, in southern Idaho on the Utah border. The lakeshores were green and peaceful, with plenty of grazing for the horses and enough game for several weeks of camping. Supply caravans arrived from Missouri with tobacco, whiskey, blankets, knives, traps, guns, and ammunition, as well as food rations. Indians, too, appeared at the Bear Lake rendezvous year after year. They brought furs and skins, which they traded for cloth, weapons, and other manufactured goods.

Some of the stories that were told at the summer rendezvous were exaggerations. But others were true, and the tale-tellers were there to prove it. Jedediah Smith really had been attacked by a grizzly bear, whose teeth had ripped his face, torn off an eyebrow, and *nearly* torn off one of his ears. Luckily, Smith was with a party of trappers whom he was leading for Ashley, and he ordered one of them to get a needle and sew his ear back on. The trapper, James Clyman, did. "I put in my needle," he later wrote in his diary, "stitching it through and through . . . as nice as I could." Despite several broken ribs, Smith recovered and his ear grew together surprisingly well.

A less fortunate case was that of another mountain man known as Peg Leg Smith (no relation to Jedediah). He was said to have been alone when his leg was shattered by gunfire. As the tale was told, he managed to amputate his own leg and also to carve a wooden one for himself from the limb of a nearby tree.

Peg Leg's story *might* have been a bit farfetched. But Jim Beckwourth's story, as told at a mountain man's rendezvous, was not. Beckwourth had been born in Virginia in 1798, the son of a white plantation owner and a black slave woman. Like so many of the off-spring of such unions, he grew up a slave. When he was in his late teens, his master took him to St. Louis and apprenticed him to a blacksmith. After a violent quarrel, he tried to run away but could find no other life for himself. In desperation, he returned to St. Louis. There Beckwourth heard of General Ashley's newspaper ad for fur trappers, and he finally saw his chance to escape. He signed up with the Rocky Mountain Fur Company, fled St. Louis, and quickly learned the skills of the frontier, becoming a resourceful scout and trapper.

The 1820s were the heyday of the mountain men. One of the things that would put an end to their way of life was a new development in men's hat fashions. In the 1830s silk began to be imported in quantity from China. It was preferred for men's tall stovepipe hats because it was lighter in weight and shinier, and considered more elegant than beaver fur.

Soon, too, the beaver streams began to be hunted out, and the mountain men went their separate ways. Many headed deeper into the West, as traders and explorers, for few were ever happy again in the more settled parts of the country. Like Jedediah Smith, Jim Beckwourth blazed trails into California for the pioneers and settlers who would follow. Beckwourth Pass in the Sierra Nevada of northeastern California is named for this courageous escapee from the life of slavery into which he was born.

JIM BECKWOURTH

Some of the mountain men, like Smith, died in their thirties. Others, like Beckwourth, who lived to be nearly seventy, had long lives of many adventures. But none would forget their years in General Ashley's company, when all had come together for a time, out of the wilderness, to the green and friendly shores of Idaho's Bear Lake.

# ILLINOIS

In the language of the Illini Indians, who were living in the region in the 1600s, the word *iliniwek* meant "men," or "people." French explorers from Canada, who were probably the first to visit the area, gave it the name *Illinois*.

The nickname *The Prairie State* best describes the landscape of Illinois. The richly fertile soil of its almost completely level grasslands grows soybeans, corn, and other crops in abundance. Another nickname, *The Sucker State,* comes from frontier days on the prairie, when thirsty travelers learned how to suck up water through long, hollow reeds from crayfish holes. Crayfish are freshwater relatives of the lobster. Although they live mainly in lakes and rivers, they also make burrows in damp meadows.

Chicago, Illinois's great city on the shore of Lake Michigan, was still a small, fortified village when the state was admitted to the Union, on December 3, 1818. After the disastrous Chicago fire of 1871, it was rebuilt, and soon its population had more than tripled. Today it is a bustling industrial and educational center, with a rich mix of people from many parts of the world.

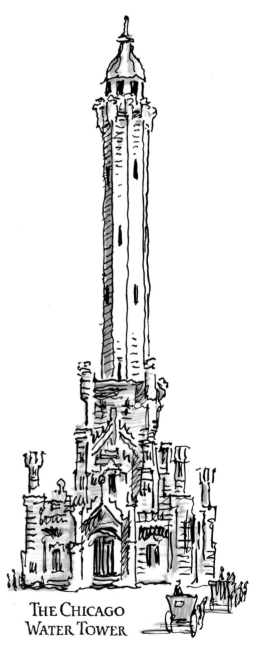

THE CHICAGO
WATER TOWER

74

**Question**: Where was the first skyscraper built, and what is the tallest building in the world today?

**Answer**: The first skyscraper, ten stories tall, was built in Chicago in 1884. The world's tallest building today is the 110-story Sears Tower, also in Chicago.

# Come to the Fair, Ride the First Ferris Wheel

In 1893 people were hearing about something called a Ferris wheel for the very first time. And what a Ferris wheel it was—not just the *first* of its kind, but a majestic, slowly turning structure as tall as a twenty-five-story building and able to carry over two thousand people at one time!

During the late 1800s, people all over America were beginning to think big. It was an exciting time, a time of fabulous inventions, such as the electric light, the Pullman sleeping car for railroad travel, and the Linotype machine, which turned out entire lines of metal printers' type. What better place to exhibit all these wonders—along with the giant first Ferris wheel—than at a huge world's fair?

Small country fairs were all very well, of course. They'd been held in America since the 1600s and were mainly for the purpose of trading livestock and selling farm products and other goods. Their entertainment was provided by clowns, puppeteers, fortune-tellers, and country fiddlers, and there were contests and races in which the fair goers took part.

A world's fair was something quite different. It announced that important things were happening in the United States. It was meant to attract visitors from all over the world. Such a fair was also known as an international exposition. Philadelphia had hosted the first successful one in the United States in 1876. It was called the Centennial Exposition because it commemorated the one hundredth anniversary of the signing of the Declaration of Independence. Inventions like the printing press, the typewriter, the telegraph, and the telephone made their bow before a fascinated public.

As the year 1892 approached, America's fair makers began to think about an exposition to commemorate the four hundredth anniversary of Columbus's discovery of America. And what better place to hold this one than in Chicago, Illinois?

Chicago was a city that had truly risen from the ashes. In 1871 a large portion of it had been destroyed in a great fire. Legend had it that the fire began when, on the evening of October 8, a cow owned by a Mrs. Patrick O'Leary kicked over a lighted kerosene lantern in a barn. Whatever the exact cause, high winds whipped the flames into an unquenchable blaze that destroyed over seventeen thousand buildings, killed three hundred people, and left nearly a hundred thousand, or a third of the population, homeless. By 1890, however, Chicago had rebuilt itself. Vigorous and fast-growing, it had a million and a half people and was second in size in the United States only to New York City.

Although the World's Columbian Exposition in Chicago was planned for 1892, it was so massive and complicated that it didn't open its gates until May 1, 1893. But what a glorious sight it was. Its buildings shone gleaming white on parklike grounds and, as the first fair to be lit by electricity, it was brilliantly illuminated at night. In addition to its machinery and arts displays, it had an entertainment promenade called the Midway Plaisance.

Here one could stroll through exhibits that re-created the splendors of Egypt, India, and the canal-threaded city of Venice. Lagoons held models of a Viking explorer ship and of the *Santa Maria* of Christopher Columbus. There was a trained wild-animal act from Germany and there were carnival sideshows of all kinds. But nothing topped the enormous Ferris wheel that loomed high above the midway. At night, when it was lit with thousands of Thomas Edison's electric light bulbs, it made the full moon look like a tiny polka dot in the sky.

The wheel had been designed by a mechanical engineer from Galesburg, Illinois, named George Washington Gale Ferris. Ferris never considered that a smaller, more portable wheel might be more

»JOHN BULL« AT THE
COLUMBIAN EXPOSITION

practical because it could be moved to other fairs or to an amusement park after the Columbian Exposition closed. He *wanted* his
wheel to be a monster, even if it had to be built in hundreds of parts
and then assembled right there at the fairground.

The foundation of the first Ferris wheel had to be sunken into a
fifteen-foot-deep bed of concrete, and it took two 500-horsepower
steam engines to turn it. Instead of having twelve to sixteen bench-
seat compartments, each holding two to three people, like most of
today's portable wheels, Ferris's wheel had thirty-six cars, each with
room for *sixty* people inside! Filled up, today's wheels might carry a
total of fifty people, while Ferris's could take 2,160.

In 1893 most people had never been higher off the ground than
a tall tree or a two- or three-story building. Imagine the thrill of
standing beneath the great wheel at the World's Columbian Exposi-

tion and waiting for it to stop at the passenger-loading platform. As you filed into the car, you tried to get close to one of the large glass windows. Then, as the wheel slowly began to lift, the very Earth beneath you seemed to be turning.

Gradually more and more of the fairground came into view. As you neared the top, you could see even farther, to the Chicago lakeshore and to Lake Michigan itself. You were 264 feet above the Earth's surface, the highest you were ever likely to get if you lived in the 1800s. And just in case you didn't believe your eyes the first time, the wheel made a second full revolution before it was time to get off.

No wonder a million and a half people rode the first Ferris wheel from June to September of 1893. It was an experience that would never be forgotten. As to the wheel itself, its makers did manage to dismantle it and to reconstruct it in St. Louis, Missouri, for the Louisiana Purchase Exposition of 1904 (which commemorated the Louisiana Purchase of 1803). But after that, the great wheel was sold to a wrecking company and demolished. It took 200 pounds of dynamite to blow it up. Then it was sold for scrap metal.

Ferris wheels for fairs, carnivals, and amusement parks are still in demand today, and many are built by the Eli Bridge Company of Jacksonville, Illinois. They come in a number of styles and sizes, and are almost always portable. But no wheel since has been able to touch the first Ferris wheel for its grandeur, its size, and the thrill of soaring skyward to see the world laid out beneath you as you'd never seen it before.

# INDIANA

CAPITAL: INDIANAPOLIS

Indiana takes its name from the Indians who were living in the region in the 1700s and 1800s. Many, like the Mohican, the Delaware, and the Shawnee, had come from the East after losing their lands to white settlers. In much earlier times—probably the 1100s and 1200s—Indians known as Mound Builders had lived in the American Midwest. They built large earthworks in a variety of shapes. Some buried their dead in these mounds. The tools, carvings, and ornaments found in the Indian mounds have told us much about their culture.

Indiana's nickname is *The Hoosier State,* and its people proudly call themselves Hoosiers. Self-sufficiency and straightforwardness are identified as Hoosier traits. But nobody really knows the origin of this word. It may come from "hoozer," an old-time English word for anything that appears to be very big.

The Indiana territory was first claimed by France, in the 1700s, but soon passed into English and then American hands. It became a state of the Union on December 11, 1816. The hog-farming, corn-growing, and dairying of Indiana's earlier days have given way to an economy led by manufacturing and the steel industry. But the state is still a major producer of popcorn and of the spearmint that flavors chewing gum.

---

**Question**: Where was the first and most famous international auto race run?

**Answer**: At Indianapolis, in 1911. The race, known as the Indianapolis 500, is still held there every year on Memorial Day weekend. Nearly half a million fans go to the track to watch the racing cars, which have to circle the speedway two hundred times to cover the five hundred miles of the race.

---

# Mr. Studebaker's Horseless Carriage

If there was one thing that John Mohler Studebaker believed in, it was the wheel. Wheels moved slowly in the America of the 1700s and 1800s. It had taken 115 years, but they had transported the Studebaker family all the way from Philadelphia, Pennsylvania, to the town of South Bend in northern Indiana.

John Studebaker's German ancestors, who called themselves the Studebeckers, had sailed into the port of Philadelphia back in 1736. In the early 1800s, his parents started to move westward bit by bit in a big, roomy covered wagon. Its belly was filled with the goods of an entire household and all the tools of John's father's blacksmithing trade.

When the Studebakers got to South Bend in 1851, they decided to stay there. True, it had muddy streets and wooden sidewalks. But it was on a small river, so it had cheap water power. And a railroad line that had just been built passed through town. John's two older brothers, Henry and Clem, opened a blacksmith shop and wagon works there the very next year.

John believed in wagons, all right, but he wasn't impressed with his brothers' new business. They got orders for very few wagons that first year, and more often they got paid in piglets or sides of beef than in money. So in 1853 John built himself a sturdy wagon and joined a wagon train heading for the California goldfields. He was nineteen years old, six feet tall, and weighed 190 pounds.

John planned to pan for gold near the rough frontier settlement of Old Dry Diggin's, which was also known as Hangtown because of the swift justice that criminals received there. But when he reached Hangtown five months after leaving South Bend, something told him to stick to the wheel. Instead of trying his luck in the surrounding hills, John went to work building wheelbarrows for the other miners. He stayed in Hangtown for five years, saved up eight thousand dollars, and headed back to South Bend. Wheels were still uppermost in his mind, and now he had the money to build his family's wagon business in Indiana into a real success.

In the years that followed, John Studebaker did just that. He began to advertise Studebaker wagons and sell them through small dealers outside South Bend. In 1861 the Civil War broke out, and the Union government needed wagons. Studebaker Brothers built army supply wagons, mess wagons, gun wagons, and ambulance wagons. In addition, there was their regular business, which ranged from light buggies and fancy carriages to heavy farm wagons and town fire-engine, police, and garbage wagons.

After the war ended in 1865, J. M. (as John Mohler Studebaker

was now called) went even farther afield. He set up a wagon sales depot in St. Joseph, Missouri, the great jumping-off place for pioneer families heading west. The Studebakers showed their carriages at the Paris Exposition of 1878. And in 1880 they even got an order from the Sultan of Zanzibar!

By the time the 1890s rolled around, the Studebaker brothers had sons and sons-in-law in the business. And these young men were beginning to come up with the strangest ideas. Suppose the horse was unhitched from the carriage and some sort of self-propelling engine was put inside instead. Experiments were already being carried out in Europe and America with "horseless carriages." If the Studebakers didn't come up with one soon, they could easily become ancient history.

*What!* the older Studebakers thundered. What sort of engine could replace a horse? If it was a steam engine, it would blow up. If it was electric, the battery would run down. And if it was a gasoline engine, it was sure to catch fire.

Still, there *were* all those rumors about a couple of youngish fellows in Michigan, a Mr. Ford and a Mr. Olds, who were starting to build horseless carriages. What did *they* know about transportation? They hadn't been wagon builders for fifty years like the Studebakers.

In spite of his doubts, J. M. told his son-in-law Fred Fish to go ahead and build some electric runabout cars. In 1902, the firm made twenty. J. M.'s wife, Mary Jane, enjoyed driving hers on er-

rands around town. But the electrics couldn't go more than thirteen miles an hour, and the real demand was for gasoline-powered autos. So Studebaker started making those in 1904.

Still, J. M. never seemed totally sold on the horseless carriage. And his old coachman, who became his chauffeur, had trouble making the big change too. Often he and J. M. had to pay farmers for run-over chickens, and once they bumped into "the south end of a cow going north." Another time J. M. got driven right *into* the bank, partway through the front door. Luckily nobody got hurt. All of this led J. M. to offer some warnings to the public about the automobile.

He admitted that it had "come to stay." But he cautioned that it was "a luxury" and that "a horse and buggy will afford a great deal of enjoyment." J. M. went on to advise those with limited money that "an automobile is a piece of machinery that has to be looked after. It is expensive and will wear out."

This was around 1910. By the time John Studebaker died in 1917, over three hundred and fifty thousand Studebaker cars were on the road, and the company had taken its place among the successful automakers of the day. Even though J. M. hadn't exactly fallen in love with the horseless carriage, Studebaker went on to produce cars in South Bend—where it gave employment to numerous workers—until 1963, when changing times in the industry forced it to close its doors.

# IOWA

A Sioux Indian people called the Ayuhwa, or "sleepy ones," are believed to have given Iowa its name. The lives of the region's Indians were peaceful indeed when the early French explorers paddled south on the Mississippi River in the 1600s. By the 1830s, though, bitter fighting was taking place between the Indians and the federal government. Sauk and Fox Indians, who'd been moved out of western Illinois to make way for white settlers, were again being pushed westward from their Iowa lands along the Mississippi.

The Sauk warrior leader was Chief Black Hawk. After his defeat in the Black Hawk War, he died on a reservation in the Iowa Territory in 1838. Out of respect for his memory, Iowa later took as its nickname, *The Hawkeye State.*

Another Iowa nickname is *The Corn State,* because Iowa's rich prairie soil has made it "the land where the tall corn grows." Since much of Iowa's corn serves as feed for livestock, the state also raises large numbers of hogs and beef cattle. Iowa was one of the states that was carved out of the vast Louisiana Purchase of 1803. It was admitted to the Union on December 28, 1846. Farming is still important in Iowa today. Manufacturing, especially of farm equipment and home appliances, also contributes to the state's economy.

---

**Question**: Which state is bounded by the two rivers that make up the longest river system in the United States?

**Answer**: Iowa. The Mississippi River forms its entire eastern boundary. The Missouri River makes up almost all of its western boundary. The Missouri then flows eastward into the Mississippi, adding up to a total length of 3,710 miles.

---

# Home Cooking, Amana Style

"If you go to Iowa," people will tell you, "you must visit the Amana Colonies." It's a little surprising to be told that there are still "colonies" in the United States, especially as far west as Iowa.

Back in 1855, though, when eight hundred or so industrious German, Swiss, and Alsatian immigrants were looking for a new home, Iowa is where they chose to settle. In a handful of years they built seven small villages, each an hour or two by ox cart from the others. The colonies were named Amana, West Amana, South Amana, High Amana, East Amana, Middle Amana, and finally Homestead.

The Amanites, as they were called, belonged to a religious group that traced its beginnings to 1714 in Germany. The word "Amana" comes from the name of a mountain mentioned in the Bible's Song of Solomon, and means "true," or "faithful." But the "true faith" of the early Amanites in Germany often made their lives difficult. Because they were totally opposed to war, they refused to serve as soldiers in the frequent fighting that took place among the individual German states.

After many years of persecution, they decided to seek out a new home in America. Following a short stay in the Buffalo area of New York State, the Amanites pushed on to the rich prairie-lands of east-central Iowa. In many ways they were like untold numbers of other ambitious, earnest, and hardworking newcomers. But in one way the Amanites were quite different. They believed that a communal way of life was their best chance of survival in the wilderness.

The members of the Amana Church Society weren't communists in the political sense. But their religion taught them that both work and its rewards should be shared equally by the entire group. All would contribute their labor according to their abilities, and all would receive food, shelter, and other necessities according to their needs.

Of course, there had to be a Council of Elders to set down the rules—and the rules were pretty strict. Everyone had to go to church eleven times a week. The women work black caps and shawls, and black aprons over their long dresses. The men dressed for church in

solemn black. The services were in German, and the hymns were sung without musical accompaniment, which was forbidden.

The rest of the time, people worked at their assigned jobs. There were farmers and flour millers; spinners and weavers; candle makers and potters; basket makers and broom makers; carpenters, blacksmiths, and wagon makers; beer brewers and butchers. Just about everything needed for a comfortable life was made by the colonists themselves and distributed among them. Money seldom changed hands.

Each family was given living quarters in part of a large house or other building. No family, however, had a kitchen, for all meals were cooked in a community kitchen and served at long tables in a common dining room. Only those who were sick or very old were allowed to have their meals brought to them.

A woman's entire life was planned for her from the time she was born. Girls left school after eighth grade and were put to work in one of the more than fifty community kitchens in the seven villages. Each kitchen prepared three meals a day and two in-between snacks for thirty to fifty people.

The workday began at four thirty A.M. with the preparation of breakfast, to be served at six. At nine a coffee break of bread, butter,

CHEESE

BUTTER

BREAD

COFFEE

molasses, and coffee was served. Lunch at noontime was the big meal of the day. It always began with soup, which had been simmering since early morning. There were many kinds—dumpling soup and pancake soup, split-pea soup and lentil soup, potato soup and barley soup, just to mention a few.

Then came more dumplings or mashed potatoes with gravy, along with boiled beef or smoked pork or sausages with sauerkraut. At three P.M. the women served another snack of cheese, butter, bread, and coffee, and then they served supper at about five thirty. All of the Amana colonists seemed to have hearty appetites. The food wasn't fancy, of course. It was just good, honest home cooking—even if it wasn't cooked at home.

An Amana woman who married and had children soon found herself back at work in one of the community kitchens. Younger children were cared for in the village kindergarten, and older ones attended school through eighth grade, six days a week. There were no school breaks except at harvest time, when the children went to work in the fields.

Everything seemed to go along pretty smoothly for nearly eighty years, with the Amana colonists sharing their work, their meals, their worldly goods, and their religious life. But beneath the surface, there was growing discontent. The Council of Elders still exercised strict control. If a young man wanted to go to high school or college, he had to get its approval. If the Council refused, there was no appeal. Young women had even less chance for any other kind of life. They *had* to remain in the community kitchens. Then, too, there were those colonists who felt they worked harder than others but had no more to show for it. That didn't seem fair. Clearly it was time for a change.

So in 1932 the Amana Society proclaimed the Great Change. Unlike the Amish people (to whom the Amanites are in no way related), the Amana colonists jumped feetfirst into the twentieth century. Almost overnight they discarded their old way of dress and began to allow forms of recreation, such as music, dancing, and card, chess, and checker playing, and competitive sports like baseball.

For the first time people could arrange to own their own homes and businesses, or work for wages. Outdoor plumbing, the horse and buggy, and the kerosene lamp soon became relics of the past. Many communal buildings, like the kitchens and some of the larger houses, were sold and converted into restaurants or inns. Some of the barns and craft shops became museums where visitors of today can still experience the flavor of the Amana past.

Once the communal kitchens were gone, though, the Amana housewives had to figure out how to go about cooking at home. Some families created a kitchen out of a spare bedroom or a wide space in the hallway. They put in a wood or kerosene stove and a homemade wooden icebox. In summer, they had blocks of stored ice, from the frozen Iowa lakes, delivered to keep their food cold.

But even with a make-do kitchen of her own, how did an Amana housewife cook a meal for only five people instead of fifty? Cutting down recipes and working with normal-size pots and pans instead of huge soup cauldrons was a real challenge. After years of preparing meals in the community kitchens, the Amana women actually felt they needed cooking lessons!

Luckily, a gas-stove salesman turned up one day in the Amana colony of Homestead and began to demonstrate his newfangled appliance, which was much more reliable than wood-or kerosene-burning stoves. To entice buyers, he offered free cooking lessons *and* a few shiny new cooking utensils thrown in.

Pretty soon the Amana home kitchens began to be furnished with modern gas stoves. You could always tell when a family had installed one because two brand-new tanks of bottled gas would suddenly sprout in the yard, just outside the kitchen window.

The gas company's cooking lessons really worked, too. "Fancy" dishes that had never been made in the community kitchens began to appear on Amana tables—stuffed peppers, salmon loaf, scalloped potatoes, and wonderful home-baked pies such as butterscotch, fresh blueberry, and rhubarb custard. Best of all, the whole family could now pitch in at Christmastime to bake the traditional cookies of honey, spice, and chocolate that everyone always yearned for. There was no question that home cooking, Amana style, had gotten to be a whole lot better.

# KANSAS

Kansas is named for the Kansa, or "people of the south wind," who were members of the Sioux family. The first Spanish adventurers, led by Francisco Coronado, arrived in 1541. They hoped—but failed—to find gold in the region. American explorers of the early 1800s thought the Great Plains so barren that they dubbed them the Great American Desert. In later years, however, Kansas was to be nicknamed *The Sunflower State*, because of its tall, golden sunflowers, *The Wheat State,* and *America's Breadbasket.*

Most of Kansas was part of the Louisiana Purchase of 1803. As the Civil War approached, it became known as "bleeding Kansas" because of the fighting between the antislavery Jayhawkers and their proslavery opponents. Kansas entered the Union as a slave-free state on January 29, 1861, only months before the outbreak of the Civil War. *The Jayhawker State,* as Kansas is also known, suffered a heavy loss of life in the Union cause.

The rough-and-ready Kansas cow towns of Abilene, Wichita, and Dodge City reached their heyday in the early 1870s. As the newly built rail lines came west into Kansas, Texas cattle were driven to these railheads to be shipped east. The cowboys and gunfighters, sheriffs and outlaws, of the colorful Kansas cow towns have inspired many stories, movies, and TV series.

SIOUX

> **Question**: Where is the geographical center of the contiguous forty-eight United States?
>
> **Answer**: In Kansas. It is marked by a stone monument two miles northwest of Lebanon, in the north-central part of the state. After Alaska and Hawaii joined the Union in 1959, the most centrally located point in the United States shifted to western South Dakota.

# Dinner with the Harvey Girls

If anything changed the face of America in the latter half of the 1800s, it was the railroad. By the late 1860s railway tracks, instead of lumbering wagons, were speeding homesteaders and other newcomers to the Great Plains and the Pacific Coast. The trains were also carrying mail and factory-made goods westward, and transporting cattle, lumber, and other raw materials from the West to the markets of the East. In 1869 the Central Pacific and the Union Pacific rail lines were joined at a point in Utah, making it possible to travel across the entire continent by train.

A rapidly chugging locomotive towing its string of cars down the track was a pretty impressive sight. In fact, most Americans had never before seen an object as large or as powerful as a steam engine, and had never heard one as noisy. The insides of most of the railway cars of the 1860s to the 1880s, though, left much to be desired in the way of comfort. Robert Louis Stevenson, the British poet and novelist, described one passenger car he traveled in on his way to San Francisco as a "long, narrow wooden box, like a flat-roofed Noah's ark." It had rows of hard wooden seats, an aisle down the middle, and a stove and a crude lavatory at both ends.

Cinders, ashes, and soot sifted in through the loose-fitting windows, and often snow as well. There were places where the rails lay unevenly on the rough roadbed, so the ride was bumpy and bone shaking. People slept in their clothes. Sometimes they brought animals on board with them. None of this was too pleasant for the passengers. But one of the biggest problems on a long, uncomfortable train ride was how to get something to eat.

In the days before most trains had dining cars, there were only two choices. You could bring along a box lunch from home for the journey. Pretty soon, of course, the train was littered with hardboiled eggshells, chicken bones, and rotting apple cores. Sometimes a newsboy came on at one of the stops selling newspapers, candy, cigars, and maybe tea or coffee from a pitcher.

The other way to get a meal was to dash off the train with a few hundred other passengers at one of the fifteen- or twenty-minute stops and join the mad rush for the station lunchroom. Sometimes it had a fancy name like a "refreshment saloon." But it was rough-and-tumble all the same. The grimy passengers had no chance to wash up. They gobbled down whatever food was offered and hurried back onto the train with their mouths full, often nursing a burnt tongue and a case of indigestion as well.

A young man who worked as a freight agent for the Chicago, Burlington and Quincy Railroad in Illinois couldn't help noticing the terrible eating facilities and the poor food that was served every time a passenger train came through. Tough meats, greasy doughnuts, and bitter coffee were the usual fare. But the lunchroom operators didn't care. In a few moments the passengers would be back on the train and whisked away to distant parts, never to return.

The freight agent's name was Frederick Henry Harvey. He'd been born in London in 1835, had immigrated to the United States around the age of fifteen, and had had some restaurant experience before the outbreak of the Civil War. Harvey began to think about setting up a really roomy, comfortable, sit-down restaurant at the depot. It would have linen tablecloths, proper silverware, courteous, uniformed waitresses, and good, wholesome food at reasonable prices. If the train conductor could get a count of the passengers who wanted to eat there and telegraph ahead to the restaurant, the meal could be all ready to serve when the train pulled in.

Harvey brought his idea to his employers at the Chicago, Burlington and Quincy Railroad. He was pretty sure they'd agree that such a restaurant would increase passenger traffic and make money on its own as well. But the managers actually laughed him off. As a joke, they suggested he try some small, struggling railroad like the Atchison, Topeka and Santa Fe Railway out in Kansas.

Fred Harvey decided to take them seriously. He did exactly that, and in 1876 he opened the first Harvey House restaurant at the railroad station in Topeka, Kansas. Imagine the delight of the first group of travel-weary passengers as they entered a station eatery that

had room for all, tables set with clean, sparkling dinnerware, and a well-cooked meal ready to be served by pleasant young women in starched white aprons. Harvey guaranteed that he would have his customers fed in a civilized manner and back on the train in thirty minutes, and he did.

Harvey girls, as the waitresses came to be known, were chosen with care from want ads placed in newspapers back East. They had to be "young women of good character, attractive and intelligent, 18 to 30." A young woman who wanted to be a Harvey House waitress went through six weeks of training before she was sent out to one of the restaurants in the rapidly growing chain in Kansas. She lived in a dormitory, often located right over the restaurant. A house mother saw that she was in by ten o'clock every evening. If she wanted to attend a dance or some other important event, she had to get a special pass.

Pretty soon prosperous farmers, ranchers, mine owners, and other lonely Kansans began riding over to the Harvey House depot restaurants to see what they were like. They were amazed at the gracious surroundings, excellent food, and attentive waitresses. It wasn't long before Fred Harvey was losing some of his best-trained young women to marriage proposals from his customers. But new recruits were always ready to come out to Kansas, "to see the world,"—as one Harvey waitress put it—and help turn part of the Great American Desert into a state that was fast becoming known for its exceptional eating places.

In 1878, two years after Fred Harvey started his Topeka restaurant, he opened a hotel near the depot at Florence, Kansas, farther down the rail line to the southwest. There, travelers could get a room for the night as well as a fine meal prepared by a chef Harvey had brought out from Chicago's famous Palmer House hotel. By the time Fred Harvey died in 1901, leaving his business to his sons, he had fifteen hotels and forty-seven restaurants, and was operating thirty dining cars on the Atchison, Topeka and Santa Fe Railway.

As the popularity of the Harvey Houses continued right through the 1920s, the crowds just never seemed to stop coming. In fact, in summer, when the largest number of trains came through Kansas, each one might discharge five or six hundred hungry travelers for a meal. Even the well-stocked Harvey kitchens sometimes began to be hard-pressed. That was when the famous whispered motto of the Harvey waitresses—"Slice the ham thinner!"—would be passed among the kitchen staff until the emergency was over.

# KENTUCKY

CAPITAL: FRANKFORT

A Cherokee Indian word, *kentake*, meaning "meadow," or "pasture," is believed to have given Kentucky its name. The gently rolling meadows of north-central Kentucky also supplied its nickname, *The Bluegrass State*. Thoroughbred horses graze the bluegrass country. The grass of this region isn't really blue. When it blooms in late May, though, it produces small blossoms that throw a dusty bluish haze over the pastures. South-central Kentucky is known for its hundreds of miles of underground passages, including Mammoth Cave, the longest in the world.

Cherokee and Shawnee Indians were living in the Kentucky wilderness when it was explored, first by French traders in the 1600s and then by Daniel Boone and other Americans in the 1700s. The Americans entered Kentucky from the east, through a pass in the Appalachian Mountain chain known as the Cumberland Gap. Settlers soon flooded the new frontier and applied for admission to the Union. Kentucky became a state on June 1, 1792.

SHAWNEE

During the Civil War, Kentucky was a border state. Although it held slaves, it never officially seceded from the Union. Some troops from Kentucky fought with the Confederate forces of the South and some with the Union armies of the North. After the war, in the 1870s, large-scale coal mining was developed in eastern Kentucky.

> **Question:** Which state was the birthplace of the two presidents who served on opposing sides during the Civil War?
> **Answer:** Kentucky. Abraham Lincoln, the Union president, was born near Hodgenville in 1809. Jefferson Davis, the president of the Confederacy, was born less than a hundred miles away, at Fairview, in 1808.

# Mammoth Cave,
# Where the Blind Fish Live

"No ray of light but the glimmer of our lamps; no sound but the echo of our own steps; nothing but darkness, silence, immensity." This was how a visitor to Kentucky's Mammoth Cave described it in the mid-1800s.

Parts of this huge underground labyrinth were first discovered by prehistoric Indians about four thousand years ago. We know this because human mummies, human footprints, and early tools and bits of clothing have been found there. They were well preserved because the temperature inside the cave, winter or summer, is always the same—fifty-four degrees Fahrenheit. Also, the humidity is quite low, and of course there is no natural light. We know, too, that the Indians who inhabited parts of the cave lit them with torches made of cane reeds, for the walls are covered with ancient soot.

Thousands of years went by during which the existence of the great cave appears to have been forgotten. Its rediscovery probably took place during the late 1700s. A Kentucky hunter and frontiersman by the name of Robert Houchins was chasing a wounded bear. The bear made straight for the cave entrance and Houchins followed. That opening, which is today known as the Historic Entrance to Mammoth Cave, led into a fantastic underground world.

In the late 1700s, however, little was known about what lay within the cave, and nobody quite knew what should be done with it. By the time of the War of 1812, the property, which was privately owned, had changed hands several times. Then, to the delight of the 1812 owners, an area near the cave's opening was found to have a rich supply of saltpeter, the largest known source of that mineral in the United States at the time. As saltpeter was essential for the manufacture of matches, gunpowder, and explosives, the cave's owners were soon doing a thriving business. During the war, they supplied enough saltpeter for four hundred thousand pounds of gunpowder with which to fight the British.

Once the war ended, however, the cave appeared to have lost its value until around 1838, when yet another owner decided to develop it as a sight-seeing attraction. Black slaves had worked the saltpeter mines in Mammoth Cave during the War of 1812. Some had ventured into the eerie channels beyond the mine works and passed on what they had learned.

So it wasn't surprising that a self-educated seventeen-year-old black slave named Stephen Bishop became the cave's first sight-seeing guide. Until his death in 1859, Bishop was famous for his daring explorations and vast knowledge of the cave's inner recesses, and for the wonderful stories with which he entertained visitors.

He and two slave guides who succeeded him, Matt and Nick Bransford, were responsible for the discovery of many of the cave's secrets. But their exploits were both difficult and dangerous. Some

STEPHEN BISHOP

of the passages they investigated were so cramped that they had to crawl on their bellies beneath a "ceiling" that was only one foot high. Others were so narrow, a normal-size person could barely squeeze through. One such passage in the cave is known today as Fat Man's Misery.

Then, as the explorers pro-  ceeded, they would find themselves in the cathedral-like room nearly two hundred feet high now known as Mammoth Dome, or on the lip of a hundred-foot-deep abyss dubbed the Bottomless Pit. In one part of the cave, called the Frozen Niagara section, are giant stone "icicles" and spires known as stalactites and stalagmites. Over millions of years, these formations dripped from the ceiling or rose from the floor. Sometimes the two join, forming draperylike columns.

Underground lakes and rivers were also found in Mammoth Cave, along with amazing varieties of fish and shellfish that adapted long ago to the eternal darkness. Eyeless fish swim in the rivers, blind shrimp and crayfish grope their way to food, and blind beetles and crickets climb the cave walls. All these species have highly sensitive bodies that make up for their lack of the sense of sight. As any experienced cave visitor knows, when the artificial lights are put out in a space that is many feet underground, there is nothing to equal the totality of the blackness.

We know today that Mammoth Cave was created by rainfall trickling through cracks in a ground surface of limestone. Slowly the water seeped through underlying layers of softer stone. When the water found levels of harder stone, it flowed along them in underground streams, opening up miles of passages. The still-changing passages are now on five different levels and go as deep as several hundred feet. But most astonishing is the fact that Mammoth Cave may be as much as five hundred miles long. Even the three hundred thirty miles that have been mapped so far make it the longest cave in the world!

In the years following the explorations of Stephen Bishop, people came up with all sorts of ideas for Mammoth Cave. In 1843 a hospital for tuberculosis patients was established inside the cave. It was believed that the unchanging temperature and humidity would help people recover from this serious infection of the lungs. Unfortunately, the experiment was a failure. The remains of the hospital, though, can still be seen in Mammoth Cave today.

Other groups decided that some of the great arching rooms of the cave, with the look of ancient temples, were the perfect setting for weddings, picnics, or theatrical events. Performances of Shakespeare's plays, with the great American tragic actor Edwin Booth, and concerts by Jenny Lind, the famous "Swedish Nightingale," were given in Mammoth Cave during the 1800s.

Since 1941 Mammoth Cave has been part of the federal government's National Park Service. A variety of breathtaking guided tours are available to visitors. They range from a one-and-a-half-hour tour for the disabled that descends into the cave's depths by elevator, to the six-hour Wild Cave tour for the hardy. This tour requires belly crawling through unlit and unimproved areas while wearing hard hats with headlamps attached. Between these extremes there are walking tours of varying lengths into different portions of the cave, including a boat ride on the Echo River, where the blind fish live.

# LOUISIANA

In the late 1600s the lands drained by the mighty Mississippi River were claimed for France by the explorer René-Robert Cavelier, Sieur de la Salle. He named them La Louisiane after the French king Louis XIV. In 1803 the territory known as the Louisiana Purchase became part of the United States. Present-day Louisiana was one of the thirteen states or parts of states carved from that territory. It was admitted to the Union on April 30, 1812.

Louisiana has a number of nicknames. It's called *The Bayou State* because of the bayous, or slow-flowing streams, that thread its marshes. It's known as *The Pelican State* for the large-billed birds that fish its waters, and *The Sugar State* for both its sugarcane-growing and its sugar refineries.

*The Creole State* refers to Louisiana's mix of early French and Spanish settlers, known as Creoles. Indian groups had been native to the region for thousands of years. And Louisiana's colorful culture was further enriched by the African heritage of its black slave population. The latter half of the 1700s saw the arrival of Cajuns, or French Canadians from Nova Scotia, originally known as Acadia. "Cajun" was a slurred way of saying "Acadian."

The city of New Orleans is especially well known for its Mardi Gras, a day of fancy-dress balls and street parades just before the fast of Lent. These festivities are actually the culmination of a long carnival season that begins on January 6. Mardi Gras was introduced by French colonists in the 1700s.

---

**Question**: In which state was a famous battle fought *after* the war itself had ended?

**Answer**: Louisiana. In January 1815, General Andrew Jackson (still fighting the War of 1812) soundly defeated the British at the Battle of New Orleans. The news of the peace treaty, signed fifteen days earlier in Belgium, had been too slow in arriving to stop the fighting.

---

# Jean Lafitte, Pirate or Patriot?

Jean Lafitte didn't *look* like a pirate. He didn't have a gold tooth or a gold earring, a long scar on his cheek or a bushy black beard, a glass eye or a terrifying hook instead of a hand. Tall, pale skinned, and soft-spoken, he always dressed neatly in well-cut black clothing. Among his friends were some of the most important figures in New Orleans society in the year 1813. They included merchants, lawyers, and wealthy planters from the nearby sugarcane plantations. Often Lafitte could be seen in the New Orleans coffeehouses quietly conducting business with some distinguished-looking gentleman.

Yet there were always whisperings about Jean Lafitte and his older brother, Pierre. They had two "business establishments" in town. One was a blacksmith shop on St. Philip Street where there never seemed to be any smithy work going on. The other was a fancy-goods shop on Royal Street that wasn't open to the public but was rumored to be stocked with the most elegant wares—rare silks and brocades, jewelry, and fine ornaments of porcelain, crystal, gold, and ivory.

Lafitte himself didn't live in New Orleans. Since 1811 he'd been

living some miles south of the city, on an island called Grande Terre, in Barataria Bay, an inlet of the vast Gulf of Mexico. Those who were invited to visit the island on business were escorted there by Lafitte's men, for the route was very tricky. One had to glide in a small boat through the "trembling prairie," a region of swamps and bayous inhabited by alligators, snakes, and other forms of wildlife. It was very easy to get lost and disappear forever in this watery landscape dotted with islands of giant moss-draped oaks.

Those who did visit Lafitte's domain on Grande Terre reported that his house was magnificently furnished and that guests were served the finest foods and wines. The other buildings on the island included warehouses and the more modest dwellings of the thousand or so men who worked for Lafitte. In the harbor were a dozen fine seagoing ships.

Where did all this wealth come from? Where did Lafitte's men and ships go when they sailed out of Grande Terre? What was in those warehouses on the island? And why did so many wealthy people have secret dealings with Lafitte? It didn't take much to put two and two together and conclude that Jean Lafitte practiced piracy on the high seas.

Governor William Claiborne of Louisiana had been charging all along that Lafitte was a pirate. But Lafitte insisted he was a privateer. There was a big difference. A pirate raided any ship for booty and treasure. A privateer was licensed by a given country to attack the ships of that country's enemy. Jean Lafitte had a license from the city of Cartagena, in Colombia, South America. Colombia was trying to throw off the domination of Spain. So, Lafitte insisted, he was legally engaged to bring in the cargoes of Spanish ships. He swore that he preyed on the ships of no other country. But Governor Claiborne didn't believe him.

The governor was so angry, in fact, that he put a price of five hundred dollars on Lafitte's head. That was the sum to be paid as a reward for his capture. This merely amused Lafitte, who turned up in New Orleans, pulled down all the governor's reward posters, and put up others offering fifteen hundred dollars—three times Claiborne's offer—for the capture of Governor Claiborne!

One of the reasons Lafitte was so cocky was that business had been

better than ever since the War of 1812 had begun to affect trade in the South. With the British Navy blockading American waters, smuggled goods of all kinds were increasingly valuable. By 1814 the British were becoming a very real threat to New Orleans. Imagine Governor Claiborne's surprise when, in September of 1814, he received a letter from Jean Lafitte offering his services in *defense* of New Orleans. Lafitte wrote that the British had approached him on Grande Terre and offered him thirty thousand dollars and a captaincy in the British Navy if he would fight on their side and lead them through the bayous to New Orleans. Lafitte even enclosed the British documents of the offer to prove he was telling the truth. But, Lafitte declared, he wanted to help the Americans instead. "I am," he wrote humbly, "the stray sheep, wishing to return to the sheepfold."

*Impossible!* Governor Claiborne thought as he read the letter. He'd been mocked and humiliated by Lafitte. There was no way he could believe that this pirate intended to become a patriot. And in a fit of rage, he commanded that Grande Terre be raided and the pirate lair scattered once and for all. Although Lafitte escaped, some eighty men and half a million dollars' worth of goods were captured. Lafitte's Barataria stronghold was all but destroyed.

But could anyone ever figure out Jean Lafitte? He was as much of a mystery as all the rumors about him. Supposedly born around 1781 in France, he'd run away to sea at the age of thirteen and had no loyalty whatever to any country. Supposedly money, pride, and personal power were all he really cared about. And supposedly he would be furious with Governor Claiborne and promptly help the British to destroy New Orleans.

Instead Lafitte did just the opposite. When the battle-weary American general, Andrew Jackson, arrived in New Orleans on December 2, 1814, Lafitte lost no time in meeting with him and repeating his offer of help in the upcoming military engagement. Short of ammunition and with a ragtag army of only two thousand men—against over eight thousand British—General Jackson accepted Lafitte's offer and had Lafitte's men released from jail. The decisive Battle of New Orleans came on January 8, 1815, with the Baratarians the heroes of the day.

A month later President James Madison issued a proclamation granting a full pardon to Lafitte and all his followers in return for the services they'd rendered to the nation. Oddly, this honor left Lafitte uneasy. Too ashamed to resume his old life in Louisiana, he set up new "privateering" headquarters in 1817, on the island of Galveston in Texas, and called his colony Campeachy. But by 1821, threatened with new charges of piracy by the United States government, he burned Campeachy and sailed away, leaving behind rumors of buried treasure all along the Gulf Coast from Florida to Texas.

Lafitte's final fate is unknown, for he was never heard from again. Some say he continued his piracy in South America. Some say he was killed in a sea battle with the British in the Gulf of Mexico. And many believe that he died of fever in Mexico in 1826. As to the question of whether Jean Lafitte was a pirate or a patriot, the answer seems to be that this strangely proud and secretive man was a little bit of both.

In 1779 Martha gave birth to the last of her nine children. She had already become a good neighbor, helping other women give birth in settlements up and down the river. It was common practice in those days for an unschooled but experienced woman, rather than a licensed doctor, to assist in childbirth. Such women were known as midwives. Today, specially trained and licensed midwives are still delivering babies. As to Martha, her skills were in growing demand as more and more settlers arrived.

We know of her midwifery because in 1785 Martha Ballard began to write a diary, which she kept until her death—at the age of seventy-seven—in 1812. During those twenty-seven years Martha recorded having delivered 816 babies. Often she was called out in the middle of a winter's night, traveling on foot or on horseback across the frozen Kennebec River and scrambling up its icy banks. In rainy weather her horse was likely to slip in the mud and throw her. And once, when the river was in flood and her horse couldn't carry her, she wrote in her diary, "I Crost the stream . . . on fleeting Loggs & got safe over."

Martha charged the equivalent of two dollars in English shillings for the delivery of a child. But often families paid her in goods rather than money. She wrote of receiving cheese, butter, piglets, turkeys, "2 lb coffee, 1 yd ribbon," and "1½ Bushl of apples . . . not very good."

Martha Ballard's practice wasn't limited to midwifery. She had never forgotten the diphtheria epidemic that had taken the lives of her three little girls. When scarlet fever struck the Maine communities in 1787, Martha nursed the sick children. She applied soothing dressings to their flushed and fevered faces and bathed the painful open sores in their throats. Martha's remedies for "canker rash," as scarlet fever was then called, were made mainly from plant roots, herbs, and berries. Many of them were grown in her own garden.

Over and over again Martha wrote, "I sett up the most of the night," as she relieved the worn and worried parents at the child's bedside. When a child died, as often happened in the days before modern medicine, Martha helped to prepare the body for burial.

Then, in the very early morning hours, she made her way home through snow drifts or thick mud, through wind, fog, or rain, as the Maine seasons dictated. Finding hardly any time to sleep and tend to

her own household chores, she was soon summoned again to attend a young victim of burns or frostbite, a case of measles or "hooping Cough," or a frightened young woman about to give birth.

For miles along the Kennebec, everyone knew that Martha Ballard made house calls. Gentle and experienced, she entered the sickroom bringing hope and easing suffering with the methods and medicines that were known to her. She risked her own health and well-being through exposure to infection and disease and through the trials of her daily travels. She witnessed the beginning of life and, all too often, she saw life end in infancy, childhood, or early youth.

Keeping a diary, as Martha Ballard did, was of great value, for this two-hundred-year-old telling of her daily life has come down to us. In 1930, Martha's great-great-granddaughter, Mary Hobart, herself a doctor, gave the fading, crudely written pages to the Maine State Library. Because Martha's family preserved her writings, we are all richer in our picture of a world long gone by.

# MARYLAND

Queen Henrietta Maria of England gave Maryland its name in 1632, when she granted the land to the first Lord Baltimore for the development of a colony. Her husband, King Charles I, had already lent *his* name to the Carolina region of North America.

Indians, mainly of the Algonquian family, lived in the area when the first English navigators appeared. The second Lord Baltimore, himself a Roman Catholic, opened the colony to Protestants as well. Maryland's "troops of the line" fought so gallantly in the American Revolution that George Washington honored Maryland by nicknaming it *The Old Line State*. Maryland joined the Union on April 28, 1788. In 1791 it gave up a portion of its territory, which became the site of Washington, D.C., the nation's capital.

After burning Washington during the War of 1812, British troops went on to attack Baltimore, Maryland's great seaport city. Its bombardment inspired Francis Scott Key's verses to "The Star-Spangled Banner." During the Civil War, Maryland remained in the Union, although it was a slaveholding state.

Maryland is divided by the Chesapeake Bay into an Eastern Shore and a larger, western region. Today manufacturing and commerce are most important in Maryland's economy. But the Chesapeake, a renowned fishing ground for crabs, clams, and oysters, still supplies a good part of the state's wealth.

GEORGE CALVERT, THE FIRST LORD BALTIMORE

**Question**: Which state held a famous race between a coal-burning steam locomotive named *Tom Thumb* and a horse?

**Answer**: Maryland. In 1830, *Tom Thumb*, designed by the American inventor Peter Cooper, ran a race with a horse near Baltimore. Although the real horse beat the "iron horse," *Tom Thumb* was promptly improved and pulled one of the first passenger trains on the Baltimore and Ohio Railroad.

# Mary Pickersgill and the Flag at Fort McHenry

We're all familiar with the *first* United States flag, with its thirteen stars and thirteen stripes, representing the thirteen American colonies. The Continental Congress approved its design in 1777. By 1792, however, the flag had to be redesigned. Two new states—Vermont and Kentucky—had been added to the first thirteen. So Congress ordered that, starting on May 1, 1795, the flag should have *fifteen* stars and *fifteen* stripes.

As the invention of the sewing machine still lay more than fifty years in the future, all flags had to be sewn by hand. There were lots of flag makers around, so nobody knows for sure who made the first fifteen-star flag.

We do know, though, that in July 1813 the commander of Fort McHenry, which guarded the inner harbor of Baltimore, Maryland, was preparing to defend it against the British, who had been threatening to attack since the start of the War of 1812. "It is my desire," the fort's commander wrote to the general in charge of Baltimore's defenses, "to have a flag so large that the British will have no difficulty in seeing it from a distance."

In due course this request was transmitted to a young widow by the name of Mary Pickersgill, who lived in a modest brick house near the Baltimore waterfront and who advertised herself as a maker of "Ships Colours, Signals, etc."

Mary Young Pickersgill was born in Philadelphia in 1776. Members of her family had known General George Washington, and her mother had made a special flag for the general's headquarters in Massachusetts. It was known as the Cambridge, or Grand Union, flag. In 1795 Mary married a young man named John Pickersgill, but in 1805 John died. Soon afterward Mary Pickersgill moved, with her mother and her little daughter, to Baltimore.

There she carried on her family's trade of making ships' banners, flags, and insignia of all sorts. Never before, however, had she received an order for a flag as large as the one that was to fly over Fort McHenry. It was to measure thirty feet by forty-two feet, the size of a large ballroom in colonial America.

It's hard indeed to imagine how Mary Pickersgill managed to handle such huge lengths of cloth, or where she found the room for them in her little house, in which she did spinning and weaving as well as sewing. The flag took many months to make. But on September 13, 1814, when the British began their twenty-five-hour bombardment of Fort McHenry, Mary Pickersgill's enormous banner was waving proudly over the garrison.

The rest of the story is familiar history. Francis Scott Key, a Washington, D.C., lawyer, was aboard a prisoner-exchange boat in Chesapeake Bay, trying to gain the release of a friend who'd been captured in Washington by the British. From this viewing point Key watched the shelling of the Baltimore fort through the night. The next morning, as the smoke and mist cleared, he was overjoyed to discover that "our flag was still there." He immediately began writing the first of the four verses of "The Star-Spangled Banner" on some paper he had in his pocket.

Although writing verse came easily to him, Key did not consider himself a poet, and he definitely was not a composer of music. He set his lines to the melody of an old English drinking song, "To Anacreon in Heaven," that was quite well known in America at the time. Anacreon was the name of an ancient Greek poet.

Within days the words to Francis Scott Key's "Star-Spangled Banner" were printed on handbills and distributed thoughout Baltimore. The song became popular at once, especially among the military. It wasn't until 1931, though, that it was officially declared by Congress the national anthem of the United States.

Today Mary Pickersgill's home in Baltimore is open to visitors and is called the Star-Spangled Banner Flag House. It looks much as it did when she sewed the largest battle flag that the nation had yet known. Preserved, too, is the original Star-Spangled Banner. It can be seen in the Smithsonian Institution's National Museum of American History in Washington, D.C. In order to shield the flag from the effects of light and dust, it is kept behind a curtain that is lowered for viewing for two minutes every hour on the half hour.

Aside from its immense size and historical importance, the flag is a rare example of a "fifteen striper." By 1817 five more states had entered the Union.

How would a flag with *twenty* stripes on it look? And what would happen as more and more states were added? The white stars on the blue background could easily be increased and rearranged as needed, but the stripes would become dizzying.

So on April 4, 1818, Congress sensibly put the number of stripes back to thirteen and ordered that they should remain that way. The stars, of course, were increased and their pattern rearranged as more states were added, to total the fifty that we have today.

# MASSACHUSETTS

CAPITAL: BOSTON

In the early 1600s an Algonquian people called the Massachuset were living near the landing place of New England's first permanent white settlers. Their name, translated as "at [or near] the great hill," was to give the state of Massachusetts its name.

Probably the first English navigator to explore the Cape Cod area of Massachusetts was Bartholomew Gosnold, in 1602. John Smith, another English sea captain, mapped the Massachusetts shoreline in 1614. But the Pilgrims' settling there in 1620 was an accident. They had been seeking a harbor much farther south when their ship was blown off course in a storm.

One nickname for Massachusetts, *The Old Colony*, refers to the early settlements of the Pilgrims and later Puritans. Massachusetts Bay is responsible for another nickname, *The Bay State*. And *The Baked Bean State* tells us of the Puritan custom of cooking baked beans on Saturday to allow time for Sunday's strict Sabbath observances.

THE SACRED COD CARVED 1760,
NOW IN THE STATE HOUSE, REPLACED AN
EVEN EARLIER VERSION

118

As the site of the Boston Tea Party and a training ground for famed regiments of minutemen, the colony of Massachusetts took an active role in the American Revolution. It became a state of the Union on February 6, 1788.

---

**Question**: Which state hung a five-foot-long wooden carving of a codfish in its Old State House in 1784, while it was still a colony?

**Answer**: Massachusetts. The cod, later moved to the Massachusetts House of Representatives, was originally mounted as a tribute to the importance of codfishing in the colony's early history.

---

# The Ice King of New England

"He who . . . despairs of success . . . has never been, is not, and never will be a hero in war, love, or business." These brave words were written by a young man from Boston, Frederic Tudor, on the cover of his diary on August 1, 1805.

Like so many New Englanders of his day, business was clearly on Frederic Tudor's mind. Long before the American Revolution, the Massachusetts colonists had realized that their soil was too rocky for large-scale farming. Their most plentiful natural resources were lumber from the forests and fish from the sea.

The sea, which had brought the people of Massachusetts to the New World, also opened the way to the world at large. For very soon they were building ships, exporting lumber, fish, and whale products, and bringing home trade goods such as spices, sugar, and cotton all the way from India, and tea, silks, and porcelain from far-off China.

Frederic Tudor, though, had an idea that went beyond the more familiar cargoes of the day. Ever since the 1700s the wealthy plantation owners of the South had been enjoying iced drinks, ice cream, and other frozen desserts in summer. The ice for these luxury foods had come from icehouses on the estates themselves. These underground storage areas were usually located near a pond or river that froze in winter. Black slaves hacked the ice into large blocks and hauled it, through narrow earth tunnels, into the icehouses. As the blocks were stacked, layers of straw were placed between them so that they could be separated easily when needed.

This ice-storage system worked well for the American South, where winters were often cold enough to bring on a freeze and slave labor was plentiful. But what about parts of the world where it was summer all year round? Frederick Tudor decided that if he could "harvest" ice from the frozen ponds of Massachusetts and ship it to the West Indies and other tropical ports, he would have found a way of extracting wealth from yet another natural resource of his home state.

The young man was especially anxious that his scheme should work. His father was a prosperous Boston lawyer, and his three brothers had attended Harvard University. But Frederic had made his mind up at the age of thirteen that *he* would become a businessman. And he did. In 1806, when he was twenty-one, he sent his first shipment of ice out of Boston. It consisted of 130 tons of freshly cut blocks of ice bound for the sugarcane-growing island of Martinique in the Caribbean Sea.

Even though most of Boston thought he was mad, Tudor was sure he had planned everything in advance. He had designed ice-storage facilities on board ship and built a specially constructed ice warehouse for his cargo on Martinique. And he had guaranteed the wealthy planters of the island a long-lasting supply of ice for their drinks and desserts and for preserving perishable foods.

But alas, Frederic was still new to the business. His icehouse could not withstand the island's tropical climate. Within six weeks the very last chip of his 130 tons of ice had melted.

As Tudor had pledged in his diary, however, he did not give up. He continued to experiment with icehouse designs, he secured exclusive rights to cut ice from certain Massachusetts ponds, and he sold the demand for ice far and wide. He conducted taste tests in warm climates to convince people that chilled beverages were more

refreshing than unchilled ones. He showed how ice could be used to reduce fevers and swellings in sickrooms and hospitals. And he shipped chilled cargoes of foods such as butter, cheese, and apples to show how fresh and wholesome they could be even after a long sea voyage.

It was not surprising that by the early 1820s Frederic Tudor's business was prospering. Instead of doubting him, the people of Massachusetts were starting to call him "the Ice King."

In 1833 Tudor tried an even more daring experiment. He sent his own ship, carrying 180 tons of ice, on a four-month journey from Boston to Calcutta, India. There it was stored successfully in an ice depot of his own design. Among his best customers were the British colonials living in India, eager for a means of cooling their household water and preserving food in the torrid climate.

Soon ice in much, much larger quantities was being shipped out of Boston to the Philippines, China, and Australia, as well as to the Caribbean and South America. Frederic Tudor had started out with a very simple idea—an idea, in fact, that most people thought was simpleminded. Yet with drive and determination, Tudor had won out. Above all he had followed the New England tradition of using thrift and enterprise to make the most of what one had.

# MICHIGAN

French missionaries and fur trappers explored this region for the first time in the 1600s. To the Algonquian Indians who inhabited it, it was known as *michi gami*, or "big water." This description suits Michigan well, for its shores are lapped by four of the five Great Lakes—Erie, Huron, Michigan, and Superior. *The Great Lakes State* and *The Water Wonderland* are two of its nicknames. One of Michigan's other nicknames, *The Wolverine State*, refers to these once-plentiful animals whose pelts were sold at Michigan fur-trading posts.

Michigan is separated, by Lakes Michigan and Superior, into two parts—a large, mitten-shaped Lower Peninsula and a smaller, northern one known as the Upper Peninsula. A four-and-a-half-mile suspension bridge was built in 1957 to join the two.

During the 1700s control of the Michigan territory passed from the French to the British to the Americans. The opening in 1825 of the Erie Canal— which helped connect the Atlantic Ocean with the Great Lakes—brought many settlers from New York and New England. Michigan was admitted to the Union on January 26, 1837.

By the early 1900s Fords and Oldsmobiles were being

1903 OLDSMOBILE

> **Question**: If a resident of Oregon is called an Oregonian, is someone who lives in Michigan a Michiganian?
> **Answer**: No. Michigan has a special name for its inhabitants. They are known as Michiganders!

built in Detroit. The city's fame as an auto-manufacturing center led to its being nicknamed Motor City, or Motown. Motown has also become the name of a style of popular music. Even though today's family car may *not* have been made in Michigan, most of America's favorite breakfast cereals still are. Since the turn of the century, the city of Battle Creek, Michigan, has been the nation's "cornflake capital."

# Breakfast from Battle Creek

In the year 1880 nobody would have believed that the tiny village of Battle Creek, Michigan, would by 1906 become the breakfast-food capital of the nation. Battle "Crick," as the local people called it, was said to be named for a disagreement between a small group of Indians and land surveyors in which, happily, no one had been seriously hurt. As there was a good water supply for powering machinery, the little town developed some flour mills and sawmills. Life was peaceful for the six thousand or so inhabitants.

Among Battle Creek's citizens was a young medical student named John Harvey Kellogg. He was one of sixteen children born to a broom maker from Massachusetts who had migrated to Michigan in the 1830s. There John Harvey was born in 1852.

All of the Kelloggs were members of the Seventh Day Adventist Church, which had established itself in Battle Creek around 1860. The Adventists had a set of beliefs based on the Old Testament of the Bible. Although Christians, they observed the Sabbath on Saturday instead of Sunday. They did not smoke or drink alcohol, they avoided pastries and other rich desserts, and above all they practiced vegetarianism. The body, the Adventists taught, was God's temple and must not receive the flesh of His creatures.

John Harvey Kellogg agreed with these teachings, for he believed that vegetarianism was also the road to good health and long life. The diet of most Americans in the latter half of the 1800s was heavy and greasy. It consisted of fatty pork and beef that often had been preserved in a salt barrel; of doughy, sweet puddings and pies, eaten hot out of the pudding pot or oven; of boiled coffee and overcooked vegetables. Most people ate too much and, in addition, they gobbled and gulped their food, for Americans were a people on the go. It was no wonder so many suffered from the "great American stomach-ache," a form of indigestion that then went by the name of dyspepsia.

As Kellogg furthered his medical studies (which had begun with a thousand-dollar loan from the Adventists), he began to specialize in the surgical treatment of the diseases of the stomach and intestines.

He also experimented with a new diet, very different from that of his early youth—before the family had embraced Adventism—when his daily breakfast had consisted of hot pancakes with bacon fat and molasses.

Living in a small, third-story room in New York City, while studying at the Bellevue Hospital Medical College, John Harvey breakfasted on seven graham crackers, an apple, and a slice of coconut. He had no way of cooking a hot cereal such as oat porridge or cornmeal mush. And it occured to him, as he later wrote, "that it should be possible to purchase cereals at groceries already cooked and ready to eat."

John Harvey Kellogg had hit on the idea that was to make him the founder of the breakfast-food industry. When he returned to Battle Creek, he began to think of a way to turn whole wheat into a precooked flake that could be eaten with milk and fruit or a little sugar.

"The Doctor," as he was now called, had a perfect laboratory. He took over the management of the Adventists' vegetarian boardinghouse, which he developed, before long, into a world-famous health resort and hospital known as the Battle Creek Sanitarium. And he was always looking for wholesome new foods to add variety to the menu.

Many of Dr. Kellogg's experiments were carried on secretly in his wife's kitchen, in the twenty-room mansion he had built in Battle Creek. He would boil up a batch of whole wheat and water, and roll it thin. Then he would attempt to scrape it into flakes and bake them in the oven. But the wheat mixture just wouldn't flake. Time after time he ended up with hard little granules that had to be soaked in liquid for hours to become edible.

Then an accident took place. Dr. Kellogg was called away from his boiled whole wheat as it lay on the rolling board. When he came back to it some hours later, he found that it flaked beautifully and, when baked, the flakes were large, thin, crisp, and delicious! The wheat, he realized, had to *stand* awhile in order to flake, a process known as tempering.

In 1895 John Harvey Kellogg's wheat flakes went on the market for sale to groceries all over the country. This first ready-to-eat flaked cereal was called Granose. Soon Battle Creek was *the* manufacturing center for other health-food pioneers. Already, Charles W. Post, a one-time patient at the Battle Creek Sanitarium, had introduced Postum, a "coffee" made from bran and molasses. And in 1906 Dr. Kellogg's younger brother, Will Keith Kellogg, introduced the history-making Corn Flakes. In that same year, C.W. Post brought out *his* version of flaked corn, later known as Post Toasties.

Although Charles W. Post died from a serious stomach ailment at the age of sixty, both John Harvey and Will Keith Kellogg lived past their ninety-first birthdays. Flaked cereal for breakfast may *not* have been the reason for the Kelloggs' long and healthy lives. But along with C.W. Post, the Kellogg brothers brought wealth and fame to Battle Creek, Michigan—and all three pointed the way toward a lighter diet for millions of people.

# MINNESOTA

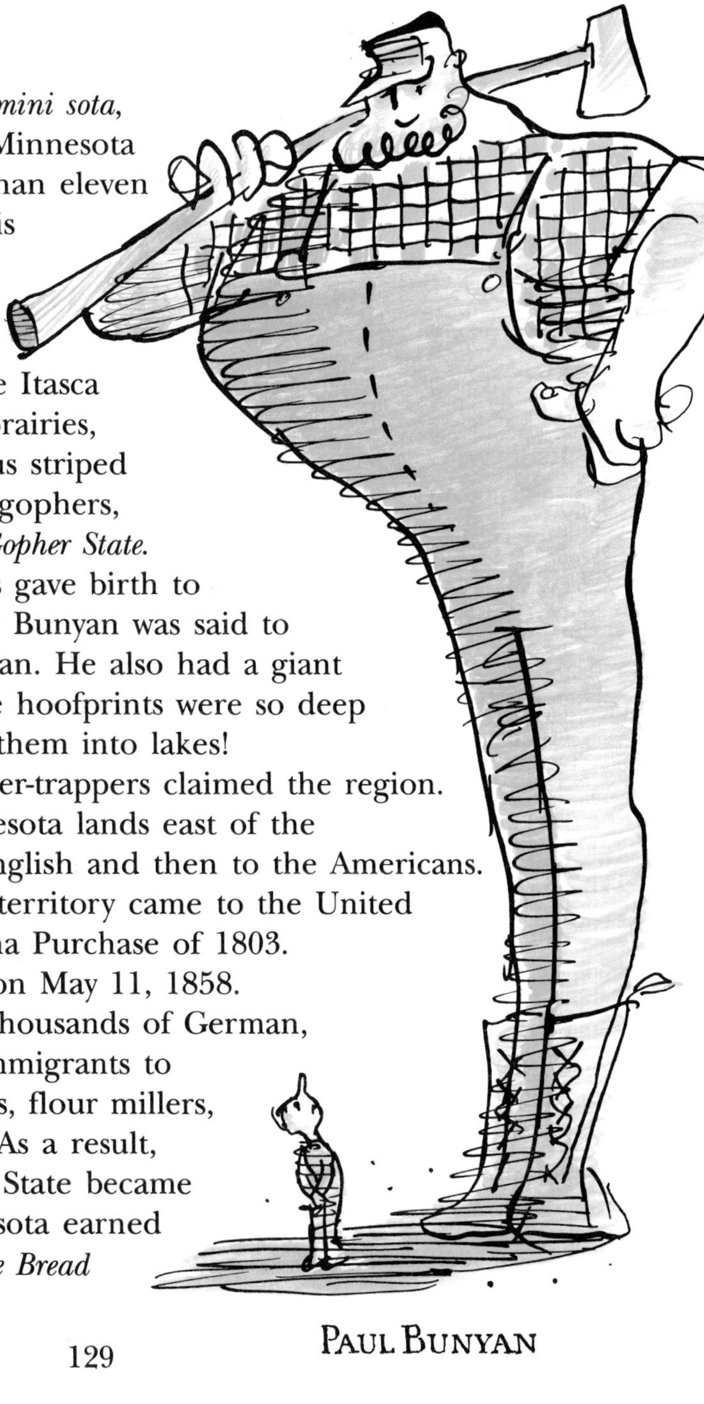

The Sioux Indian words *mini sota*, or "sky-tinted water," gave Minnesota its name. A land of more than eleven thousand lakes, Minnesota is also the state where the mighty Mississippi River rises. It starts as a shallow stream trickling out of Lake Itasca in the north. Minnesota's prairies, once inhabited by numerous striped ground squirrels known as gophers, gave it the nickname *The Gopher State*. And Minnesota's tall forests gave birth to the legend of Paul Bunyan. Bunyan was said to be a superhuman lumberman. He also had a giant blue ox named Babe whose hoofprints were so deep that melting snows turned them into lakes!

In the 1600s French trader-trappers claimed the region. But in the 1700s the Minnesota lands east of the Mississippi passed to the English and then to the Americans. The rest of the Minnesota territory came to the United States through the Louisiana Purchase of 1803. Minnesota became a state on May 11, 1858.

The late 1800s brought thousands of German, Norwegian, and Swedish immigrants to Minnesota as wheat growers, flour millers, and raisers of dairy cattle. As a result, the prairies of the Gopher State became rich farmlands, and Minnesota earned a brand-new nickname, *The Bread and Butter State*.

PAUL BUNYAN

129

A HANDSOME CARRIAGE ...

By 1860 there were twelve thousand Scandinavians in Minnesota. By 1870 Minnesota had more Norwegians and Swedes than any other state! Some had moved west from Illinois, Wisconsin, and other parts of America. But the tide was really swelled by those who came from the old country. The Norwegian and Swedish governments tried passing laws to keep debtors and those owing military service from leaving. But nothing worked.

A Swedish-born official named Hans Mattson became the general manager of the Minnesota Immigration Board. He worked hard to help "the poor immigrant . . . just landed from a steamer . . . with his wife and a large group of children around him . . . bewildered, ignorant and odd-looking." The next step was for the men of the family to find work—as farm, railroad, or construction laborers—so they could buy a farm of their own. The women, meanwhile, took in washing or worked as servants.

Perhaps it was the democratic way of life that gave so many newcomers the courage to go on in the face of hardships. Unlike the countries of Europe, America had no king and no inherited aristocracy. By the 1890s two men of Scandinavian stock had risen to the highest state office in the country. Knute Nelson, a Norwegian-American, became governor of Minnesota in 1892, and John Lind, a Swedish-American, became governor of the state in 1898.

John Johannson, a Swedish immigrant of the 1850s, seemed to have said it all in an "American letter" when he wrote, "I have now been on American soil for two and a half years and . . . my cap [is not] worn out from lifting it in the presence of gentlemen. There is no class distinction between high and low, rich and poor, no make-believe, no 'title sickness,' or artificial ceremonies."

To the Scandinavian immigrants in Minnesota, the promise of America had fulfilled itself.

. . . A WHEELBARROW

# MISSISSIPPI

CAPITAL: JACKSON

Like the river for which it is named, "Mississippi" comes from the language of one of the early shore-dwelling Indian peoples. They called it *misi* ("big") and *sipi* ("river"). The region of the state of Mississippi was inhabited by Chickasaw, Choctaw, and Natchez Indians when gold-seeking Spaniards arrived in the 1500s. Disappointed at finding no gold, the Spaniards withdrew and were replaced by the French in the 1600s and the English in the 1700s. As settlers came from the East to claim its fertile lands, the area's Indian peoples were pushed westward, mainly into the Oklahoma territory. Mississippi became a state of the Union on December 10, 1817.

Mississippi's flowering trees and shrubs, which graced many of its pre–Civil War plantation houses, gave it the nickname *The Magnolia State*. Mississippi seceded from the Union in January 1861 and fell to Union forces on July 4, 1863, after the forty-seven-day siege of Vicksburg. The state's wealth, based on slave labor, was destroyed, and Mississippi was faced with a bitter struggle for racial equality.

Today cotton and other agricultural crops, as well as shrimping and catfish farming rank alongside industry in Mississippi's economy. Another nickname, *The Mud Cat State*, refers to the famous Mississippi catfish, which has whiskers like a cat and wallows in muddy river bottoms. Catfish can weigh thirty pounds or more and make good eating at an old-fashioned Southern fish fry. Another favorite food from Mississippi is mud pie.

MAGNOLIA

134

> **Question**: This one's an old-time riddle: What has four eyes and runs over two thousand miles?
>
> **Answer**: The M*iss*iss*i*pp*i* River. The Mississippi is actually 2,340 miles long.

# How Mississippi Mud Pie Got Its Name

The Mississippi River has been called all sorts of names, some of them not very flattering. This is because Old Man River, or Big Muddy, is a powerful giant that seems to have mind of its own. The lower portion of this river has a way of meandering off into unexpected places. It can cut itself a new channel on fairly short notice, leaving a sandbar sitting high and dry in the middle of the stream. Or it can decide to flow inland and then out again, leaving behind a chain of large, U-shaped ponds known as oxbow lakes.

The farther south the Mississippi flows, the more mud it carries with it and the browner its waters get. Mississippi mud is made up of topsoil and silt, or fine, rocky particles. Much of this mud gets deposited in the riverbed, at times making the river high enough to overflow the levees, or earthen embankments, built to contain it. In years when there's been a lot of snow or rainfall in the river's area of drainage, it can descend on its lower banks in a raging flood.

This was what happened in the spring of 1927. One of the hardest-hit places in the state of Mississippi was the longtime river port of Greenville. Old Man River washed right over the levees and poured into town. It swept away houses and stores, barns and livestock, and anything else that was in its path, carrying all of it swiftly downstream.

People, too, were caught in the flood. Those who escaped the river's fury had to leave town, for all of Greenville remained underwater for seventy days—more than two whole months. And where the water *had* drained away, there was nothing but mud—shiny, pale-brown mud, oozing in all directions. As the old-time river residents

Louis, Missouri, a fitting memorial to Thomas Jefferson, Lewis and Clark, and all those others who'd played a vital role in the western expansion of the nation? The answer was a resounding *no!*

A group of St. Louis citizens formed a committee to build a proper memorial on the site and, although the United States was in the depths of a severe economic depression, President Franklin D. Roosevelt agreed that the federal government would contribute nearly seven million dollars toward the project.

More years went by, because nobody could decide what sort of memorial should be built or what should be done with the buildings that already lined the river-front. Should there be a museum dedicated to the theme of western expansion, a spacious park with pools and fountains, a colossal statue of Thomas Jefferson, or all three? Nothing seemed quite right.

At last, in 1947, it was decided that a contest should be held. Any architect who was an American citizen could submit a design for the memorial. Five semifinalists would be chosen, each to receive ten thousand dollars in prize money. The one who was selected as the final and overall winner would receive forty thousand dollars.

When the competition closed, 172 designs had been entered. Two of the competitors belonged to the same family. They were Eliel Saarinen, a very famous Finnish-born architect, and his not-quite-so-famous son, Eero Saarinen. Eero was thirty-seven years old at the time. Although he showed great ability, his successes had been overshadowed by those of his father. "I admit frankly," Eero had once written to a friend, "I would like a place in architectural history."

In planning his design for the memorial to Thomas Jefferson and

EERO SAARINEN

westward expansion, Eero kept two things in mind. He remembered how, in Washington, D.C., the Washington Monument was in the form of a vertical or upright line, the Lincoln Memorial was a cube, and the Jefferson Memorial a dome. The dome gave him the idea that a similar curved shape, such as an arch, would be suitable for the Jefferson memorial to be built in St. Louis. At the same time, a soaring arch would be a symbol of the entrance, through Missouri, to the vast western lands—truly a Gateway to the West.

WASHINGTON          JEFFERSON          LINCOLN

In September 1947 the competition jury selected Eero Saarinen as one of the five semifinalist winners for his design of a "gateway" arch. A telegram was sent to the architectural firm of Saarinen, Saarinen and Associates in Bloomfield Hills, Michigan. But through an error it congratulated *Eliel* Saarinen, Eero's father.

For three days family, friends, and fellow architects celebrated Eliel's winning of the first stage of the contest. Then the mistake was corrected. It was Eero who had won. The design that Eliel had submitted hadn't even made it to the five semifinalists' stage.

The jury reassembled on February 17, 1948, to pick the winner of the first prize. Eero won by a unanimous vote for the vision he had shown in designing his truly magnificent arch. Now the younger Saarinen came into his own. He would design many other handsome and intriguing structures before his death following brain surgery, in 1961. He was not even to see his Gateway Arch completed. Problems of clearing the site, raising the necessary additional funds, and constructing the Arch and its surroundings meant that the memorial was not finished until 1965.

Today the Gateway Arch of the Jefferson National Expansion Memorial in St. Louis, Missouri, is both an optical riddle and a delight-

ful surprise to visit. Of gleaming stainless steel, it rises in a slender curve to a height of 630 feet, about that of a 60-story building. Our eyes tell us that the arch is much taller than it is wide. But actually the distance from leg to leg is also 630 feet!

The other secret of the Gateway Arch is that it is hollow. Inside its silvery skin are two 8-car trains, one in each leg, that carry visitors to an observation platform at the top of the Arch. The five-person cars are cleverly designed to rotate so that passengers remain upright as they ride slowly through the curving channel.

From the narrow windows at the top of the Arch, one can view the grounds of the memorial park, which cover the original site of the St. Louis settlement. Handsomely restored historic buildings and the towers of the modern city blend the past and the present. A nearby landmark is Busch Stadium, home of the St. Louis Cardinals.

Although it may be hard at first to see the connection between a United States president of the early 1800s and Eero Saarinen's twentieth-century Arch, it does exist. For it was the vision of Thomas Jefferson that spurred pioneers to trek into the American heartland beneath an arching sky long before this symbolic structure was built.

# MONTANA

Partly in the Great Plains, partly in the Rocky Mountains, Montana takes its name from the Spanish word *montaña*, meaning "mountain." This fourth-largest state (after Alaska, Texas, and California) is known as both *The Bonanza State* and *The Treasure State* because of its mining riches. Gold, silver, copper, lead, zinc, and even sapphires have been found in Montana. Because of the rugged terrain of the Big Sky country, Montana has also been dubbed *The Stubtoe State*.

Both plains and mountain Indians hunted in the Montana region when French traders passed through in the 1700s. Lewis and Clark explored the area on their way to the Pacific Coast in 1805, and again on their return journey in 1806. Fur trapping, gold prospecting, and cattle raising followed. By the late 1800s the buffalo had disappeared from the plains and the Indians had lost their hunting grounds to cattle and sheep ranchers. Montana was admitted to the Union on November 8, 1889.

It's been said that there are four times as many cattle and twice as many sheep in Montana as there are people. Even today, the state's population is under a million. Tourism is an important part of Montana's economy too, as visitors are drawn to its scenic wilderness. Glacier National Park, with its more than fifty glaciers, is in northwestern Montana, and a portion of Yellowstone National Park lies on its southern border.

JEANNETTE RANKIN

146

**Question**: Which state sent the first female representative to the United States Congress?
**Answer**: Montana. In 1916, Jeannette Rankin, born near Missoula, Montana, in 1880, became the first woman in the world to be elected to a national lawmaking body.

# Miss Fligelman's Mother Was Shocked

On May 2, 1914, twenty-three-year-old Belle Fligelman of Helena, Montana, did a very "unladylike" thing. She piled into an open car with several other women who rode up and down Helena's main street, tooting on horns, waving flags, and tossing printed notices out to the crowd. Then she jumped out of the car onto a corner of the main street and proceeded to give a speech demanding voting rights for women to an audience of miners, ranchers, and other astonished passersby.

What was Belle Fligelman thinking of to behave this way in public? In the early 1900s, young women were supposed to be soft-spoken and retiring at all times. Besides, Helena still showed traces of once having been a gold-mining camp. True, the town had a railroad station, a western-style opera house, and a dancing school. But its main street was called Last Chance Gulch, because a group of discouraged prospectors had found gold in that very spot in 1864. Even in 1914, street fights were not unlikely to break out among its quick-tempered and armed male citizens.

Yet Belle's parents, Minnie and Herman Fligelman, Jewish immigrants from Romania, had come to live in Helena in 1889. Herman operated the town's dry-goods store and Minnie gave birth to two daughters, Frieda and Belle. But Minnie died soon after Belle was born, in 1891. A while later, Herman married a German-Jewish woman named Getty Vogelbaum, and so the girls grew up with a stepmother.

Getty wasn't mean or unloving, but she did have fixed ideas about

how young women should behave, and Belle's antics drove her crazy. It had begun with the argument about finishing school or college. Getty felt that Frieda and Belle should be sent away for a year or two to a finishing school, an academy that gave young women a smattering of French and other cultural studies while teaching them the niceties of social behavior. Both sisters objected strongly and insisted on a real college education, even if they had to work their way through.

Herman finally gave in over Getty's objections, and Belle went off to the University of Wisconsin. She took a degree in journalism, came back home in 1913, and got a job as reporter on the town newspaper, the *Helena Independent.*

Montana was in the midst of a women's suffrage (right-to-vote) campaign led by the energetic and electrifying Jeannette Rankin. The United States Constitution had left the question of voting rights for women up to the states. During colonial times New Jersey had allowed a woman to vote provided she was a free person and was worth fifty pounds or more. But in 1807, twenty years after it had become a state, New Jersey took the vote away from women. In 1869, however, the Wyoming Territory broke new ground by giving women the vote. Several states followed in the 1890s, so why not Montana?

Belle Fligelman was less than five feet tall. But she didn't let that stop her. On that May afternoon when she made her first street- corner speech, she simply jumped up onto a box. She knew, of course, that her stepmother would disapprove. So that night she checked into a hotel and charged the cost of the room to her father. Getty was deeply shaken. What young woman slept away from home in her very own town? After that, Belle was allowed to speak on street corners or from the backseat of an open car, as long as she returned home by evening.

That summer Belle and other Montana suffragists made horse-and-buggy trips to the gold-mining towns and ranching communities some distance from Helena to campaign for the women's vote. When Belle's stepmother heard about how Belle had danced with the miners after giving a talk in the Miners Hall in Marysville and lectured the ranchers of Augusta in front of the town saloon, she was truly shocked.

It wasn't that Getty was against women having the vote. She firmly believed in working hard for a cause. She herself was known for driving about town in a buggy, collecting food, clothing, and money for the immigrant Jews who were arriving from Russia. It was just that Getty felt Belle's kind of politicking was out-of-bounds for a lady.

At last November came, and the Montana voters (men only, of course) went to the polls to decide whether the state should give women the vote. Everyone waited anxiously for days until all the ballot boxes were opened and the ballots counted. There were plenty of antisuffragists in Montana, including women who felt that "mixing in politics" was "a man's job." They didn't see, even after Jeannette Rankin patiently explained it, that without the vote women had nothing to say about many matters that touched them directly, such as the health and welfare of their children and the labor conditions in the factories where they worked.

To the suffragists' great joy and relief, the women's voting rights amendment to the Montana state constitution did pass, by a margin of four thousand votes! But if Belle's stepmother thought Belle was now going to settle down and perhaps start looking for a husband, she was much mistaken. Having finally gotten the vote, Montana women felt it was time to do something important with it.

The next step, in fact, was to get Jeannette Rankin, the inspired leader of the suffrage movement, elected as the state's representative to the United States Congress. Once again Belle, the "plucky little generalissimo," as she was called, took her place in the front ranks of the campaign. Once again Getty was horrified. And once again the campaign was a success.

In November 1916, Jeannette Rankin was elected. And in April 1917, when she took her seat as the first woman in Congress, Belle went along to Washington, D.C., with her to serve as her assistant. One of the greatest achievements of Jeannette Rankin and her supporters was the passage of the Nineteenth Amendment to the United States Constitution. This *national* suffrage law went into effect in August 1920, giving women throughout the country the right to vote.

In the end, Getty got her way—more or less. In 1918, while Belle was working in Washington, she met and married a young Yale graduate named Norman Winestine. In 1921 Belle, her husband, and their two little daughters returned to Helena to live.

Belle never gave up, though, on her efforts to improve the lives of women and children. She worked for the League of Women Voters, for a national child labor law, and for the right of women to serve on juries. She went out to ring doorbells for all sorts of good causes, and she never hesitated to take all her children along, including her little boy Henry, who'd been born after her return to Helena. If Belle's stepmother thought *that* was unbecoming conduct for a wife and mother of three, so be it.

When in her eighties, Belle Fligelman Winestine, still active and still living in Helena, Montana, wrote her story, "Mother Was Shocked," for *Montana: The Magazine of Western History.*

# NEBRASKA

Nebraska takes its name from an Oto Indian word that translates as "flat water." This was how the Oto, a people of the Sioux, described the shallow Platte River, which runs the entire width of the present-day state.

Starting in the 1840s, wagon trains heading for Oregon and California followed the broad valley of the Platte River westward. Few people thought of settling on the dry plains of what was then known as the Great American Desert. Nebraska was merely a place one traveled through on the way to someplace else. It wasn't until the passage of the Homestead Act of 1862, with its promise of free farmlands, that settlers began to arrive.

Statehood came for Nebraska on March 1, 1867. But it took many years for farmers to overcome the hardships of the unbroken prairie and for Nebraska to earn its nickname, *The Cornhusker State.* Today corn is still Nebraska's main crop. Wheat is second, and there is also a large livestock industry.

**Question**: In which state was the first Arbor Day celebrated?
**Answer**: Nebraska, in 1872. Nebraskans realized that planting trees would conserve moisture, enrich the soil, and bring welcome shade in summer. Over a million trees were planted in Nebraska on the first Arbor Day.

# Ugly as a Mud Fence

*Ten miles to the nearest water,*
*Twenty miles to the nearest tree,*
*Thirty miles to the nearest house,*
*Grasshoppers aplenty . . .*
*Gone back East to the factory.*

This verse of the 1870s from the treeless prairies of Nebraska described the discouragement of the pioneers who *didn't* stay. They gave up because the prairie grass was too tough and the soil was too dry. They gave up because swarms of grasshoppers frequently darkened the sky, as during the great plague of 1874, when they ate every scrap of plant life and even devoured clothing, mosquito netting, and wooden plow handles! Would-be settlers gave up because of blizzards, tornadoes, prairie fires, and unbearable loneliness.

Yet many of the pioneers who arrived to settle on the unbroken plains did remain. The Homestead Act of 1862 had promised them free ownership of 160 acres of farmland if they lived on it for five years and improved it. Once the Civil War ended, in 1865, Easterners, European immigrants, and Southern blacks began to trek westward and northward into Kansas, Nebraska, and the Dakotas.

Most of the black homesteaders were former slaves. Freed though they now were, they were still oppressed in most parts of the South and some parts of the North. Many worked for their old masters for poor wages. They were not permitted to vote or to mix freely with whites. In 1879 two former slaves—Henry Adams and Benjamin "Pap" Singleton—led an "Exodus" of blacks to Kansas. Other "Exodusters," including 150 blacks from Mississippi, moved north to Nebraska. Southern whites tried to stop the migration because of the loss of cheap labor. And the new communities were not always welcoming of the black settlers. But most Exodusters stuck it out.

For whites and blacks, Americans and Europeans, sticking it out meant, first of all, building a shelter. Because there were no trees on the prairie, there was no wood. So the newcomers cut up large blocks of sod—consisting of chunks of grass, tangled roots, and prairie soil—and heaped them on top of one another like bricks. A hillside or a slight rise in the ground made it easy to hollow out a sort of cave and face it with a wall of sod bricks. But most of the prairie was flat, stretching away endlessly and even terrifyingly in all directions, like the sea. So many a sod house had to be built with four standing walls.

Its roof was made of thatched grass, supported by a few precious wooden poles. Its floor was just packed earth with maybe a rug or two of buffalo hide or bearskin. Windows might be mere chinks in the wall, and the door was a heavy piece of cowhide. Deer antlers fastened to the wall made a convenient clothes rack. Most "soddies" were so small, it was hard to get the furniture *and* the family inside at once. So, often, the beds were put outside during the day and the table at night.

Rain was always welcome for planting. But it was a disaster for the

family's shelter. It turned the sod to mud and washed down the walls, leaving stalks of grass and twisted roots sticking out in all directions. This was when the sod house became "ugly as a mud fence" and had to be rebuilt. *If* times had been good and the family had prospered, it might be rebuilt with wood hauled by rail from the East. But more often than not, in the early years, the house was repaired with more sod, or what the homesteaders jokingly referred to as "Nebraska marble."

In wet weather or dry, bugs, mice, snakes, and other creatures that lived in the soil lived in the sod house with the settlers. Women worked constantly to try to keep the dirt house clean, to wash and sew, cook and make soap and candles, and feed the livestock. But no matter how busy they were all day, the emptiness of the plains, the absence of near neighbors, cast an eerie spell at night. Children often had to walk a long way to school and were sometimes the fatal victims of sudden windstorms or snowstorms.

Yet the Nebraska homesteaders tamed millions of acres of stubborn earth. And they even managed to develop a sense of humor about their surroundings. After some good years of rain during the 1870s, drought returned to Nebraska in the 1880s. The story began to go around about how one farmer on the thirsty plains somehow got hit by a drop of water and promptly fainted. The only way his family could get him to come to was by throwing several buckets of *dirt* in his face!

# NEVADA

*N*evada is the Spanish word for "snow covered." The mountains known as the Sierra Nevadas loom high on Nevada's western border. They keep out moisture-carrying clouds from the Pacific, making Nevada the state with the least amount of average rainfall. One of Nevada's nicknames, *The Sagebrush State*, describes its desertlike landscape dotted with these gray-green shrubs.

Indian groups who were cave dwellers and basket makers are believed to have lived in this region ten thousand or more years ago. Francisco Garcés, a Spanish friar on his way from Mexico to California, passed through in about 1775. He was probably the first European visitor. Fur trappers and explorers from the East began to track the region's highlands and rivers in the 1820s, searching for game and for routes to California.

In 1859 Nevada's population was swelled by the discovery of the Comstock Lode, a mining deposit rich in silver and gold. Nevada then became known as *The Silver State*. Its newfound wealth and the fact that it was slave free made it an attractive candidate for statehood during the Civil War. *The Battle Born State* (still another nickname) was admitted to the Union while the war was still raging, on October 31, 1864. In the early 1900s, after years of mining booms and busts, Nevadans turned to irrigated cropland and sheep raising as more reliable sources of income. The state also began to attract visitors by offering liberal divorce laws, and by legalizing gambling in 1931. Today Las Vegas is Nevada's biggest lure for those seeking entertainment and luck at the gaming tables.

---

**Question**: Which is the seventh largest state but has the sixth smallest population?

**Answer**: Nevada. It has fewer than one million permanent residents.

---

# Sam Clemens Changes His Name to Mark Twain

"It never rains here, and the dew never falls. No flowers grow here, and no green thing gladdens the eye. The birds that fly over the land carry their own provisions with them."

These were the words of young Sam Clemens in a letter from Carson City, Nevada, to his family back home in Hannibal, Missouri. It was August of 1861, and twenty-five-year-old Sam and his brother Orion had only just arrived, covered with dust, in the Nevada Territory. They'd traveled west by stagecoach all the way from St. Joseph, Missouri—a twenty-day journey of about eighteen hundred miles.

But long-distance travel, even the slow kind of the mid-1800s, had never bothered Sam Clemens, as long as there was some adventure in it. He'd already left home in his teens to work as a printer's assistant and sometime journalist. He'd spent time in New York, Philadelphia, and Washington. Then, longing for even more distant parts, he'd boarded a Mississippi River steamboat bound for New Orleans. From there, Sam intended to find a ship that would take him to South America for a look at the Amazon River country.

Somehow, though, Sam got caught up with the Mississippi River instead. He decided it would be a great adventure to learn the river, with its tricky reefs and sandbars, and its menacing, changing channels that could ground and destroy a large steamboat. Sam worked as an apprentice for two years, got his river pilot's license, and piloted paddle wheelers up and down the Mississippi for the next two years, from 1859 to 1861.

By then it was time for something new. So when Sam's older

brother Orion was appointed secretary to the governor of the newly created Nevada Territory, Sam went along as the secretary's secretary. No sooner had he arrived in the scrubby desert outpost of Carson City than he decided to try his luck at mining for silver, gold, or whatever else lay in the Nevada hills some two hundred miles to the north. So off Sam went, with three other prospectors, to the Humboldt River country to join all the other treasure seekers of the moment. They staked claims by the dozen and filled their pockets with rocks that hinted at "specks of gold" and "streaks of silver." But as Sam wrote, "our credit was not good at the grocer's."

Once more it was time for a change. So back Sam came from the hills, this time to Virginia City, about twenty miles northeast of Carson City. Virginia City had sprung up on the site of the famous Comstock Lode, the bonanza gold and silver strike of 1859. All the good claims had been taken while Sam was still a river pilot on the Mississippi. But there *was* work to be had in Virginia City, where Sam found a job as a reporter on Nevada's first newspaper, the *Territorial Enterprise.*

NOBODY KNEW ANYTHING

The only problem was that there wasn't all that much news to report. Even though Sam wandered around town all day asking questions, he found that "nobody knew anything." So he decided to make up some news. He made up one story about a "Petrified Man," a sort of human stone mummy, and it went over so well that other newspapers picked it up.

Sam was so delighted that he wrote another story. This one was about a bachelor who murdered his wife and nine children in a stone mansion on the edge of a pine forest just outside Carson City. Since a bachelor couldn't have had a wife, and there were *no* stone mansions in Nevada or pine forests near Carson City, Sam's story was just as farfetched as the "Petrified Man." But again everyone enjoyed it tremendously.

Since Sam signed his straight news copy (which he found so boring) Samuel Clemens, he figured he ought to find a pen name for his humorous tall tales. He didn't have a hard time thinking one up. In Sam's river-pilot days, the Mississippi channels had to be tested frequently to make sure the water wasn't too shallow. A crew member, called a leadsman, would cast a long line with a chunk of lead on the end of it into the river. If he called out, "By the mark twain," everyone knew the water at that point was "twain," or two fathoms deep. Two fathoms was twelve feet and thus safe for passage.

So Sam, who loved change anyway, signed himself Mark Twain for the first time in a bit of fanciful reporting for the *Enterprise*, on February 3, 1863.

The new name stuck. But Sam didn't. The next year he left Nevada and embarked on a life of traveling, lecturing, and writing that would make him world famous— as Mark Twain. He did leave something behind in Nevada, though. Long after his departure, the Virginia City *Enterprise* carried on Mark Twain's tradition of making up wild and funny stories any time the news itself just wasn't all that interesting.

# NEW HAMPSHIRE

**STATE CAPITOL**

John Mason, from the county of Hampshire in England, was granted a portion of New England territory in 1629. He named it New Hampshire. Earlier in the 1600s, both English and French navigators had explored the region's coastal area. They found groups of Algonquian Indians living there, hunting and growing maize and other crops during the short summers.

New Hampshire is nicknamed *The Granite State* because of the vast sources of red and gray granite found in the White Mountains in its northerly half. Mount Washington (6,288 feet) is the tallest of the White Mountain peaks and also the highest in the Northeast. In winter it is covered with about fifteen feet of snow. But in summer, weather permitting, the summit can be reached by auto road or cog railway, offering a view of Maine, Vermont, Quebec, and the Atlantic Ocean. New Hampshire itself has the shortest coastline of any state bordering on an ocean. Its Atlantic shoreline is only thirteen miles long.

Like Maine, New Hampshire was allied with the Massachusetts colony for a time in the 1600s and 1700s. However, it adopted its own constitution during the American Revolution and became a state of the Union on June 21, 1788.

---

**Question**: In which state has one of the world's highest wind velocities been recorded?
**Answer**: New Hampshire. In April 1934, the wind at the summit of Mount Washington blew at 231 miles per hour!

---

# Laura Bridgman, Out of the Darkness

*I sat down in [a] room, before a girl, blind, deaf, and dumb. . . . Her face was radiant. . . . Her hair [was] braided by her own hands . . . ; her dress, arranged by herself, was a pattern of neatness and simplicity. She was . . . writing her daily journal. Her name is Laura Bridgman.*

These words were written by the famous British author Charles Dickens after a visit to America in 1842. They appeared in a book called *American Notes,* which told of his varied experiences in the United States.

Who was this surprising young person named Laura Bridgman? She was a twelve-year-old girl when Charles Dickens met her and might never have become known to him or to others if not for a chain of happenings, some tragic and some fortunate.

Laura Bridgman was born on a farm near Hanover, New Hampshire, on December 21, 1829. Although she was a delicate little baby, she was normal in every way. She could see and hear, smell and taste, just like other children and was beginning to speak words by the time she was two.

Then, as often happened before the discovery of inoculations and antibiotics, an epidemic of scarlet fever broke out. Among those stricken were the children of the Bridgman family. There was little that desperate parents could do for a child with a serious infection.

Laura's two older sisters died of the disease. Laura herself lay burning with fever. When at last it passed, she was so weak that she could not walk for a very long time.

But something much worse had happened to Laura. Gradually her parents discovered that she could not see or hear, and that even her senses of taste and smell had been almost completely destroyed by the illness. No longer able to hear people's voices, Laura could not learn to speak in the normal way that children do. So in addition to being deaf, she was also "dumb," a word that in this case meant mute, not dull or stupid. The only one of the five senses left to Laura was her sense of touch.

What could Laura's busy parents do for her? After Laura's illness two little brothers were born, and her mother had to care for them. She also had many household chores—spinning and weaving, soap and candle making, baking, scrubbing, washing, and ironing. By the time Laura was seven, she had learned to knead dough for bread. She could spin, sew, and knit a little, and she could set the table. By feeling the shapes of the slightly dented plates, spoons, and forks, Laura knew exactly where to place each setting.

Often Laura sat in the rocking chair by the fire, stroking the family cat. But she was also eager to learn as much as she could about the world around her. If visitors came, she felt their faces with her busy, fluttering fingers so that she could recognize them when they came again.

One such visitor was a young student from Dartmouth College, in nearby Hanover. His name was James Barrett, and he often visited the Bridgman farm to do record keeping for Laura's father, who served as a selectman, or town official, for Hanover.

James Barrett was so impressed by Laura's quickness and intelligence, and so saddened by her bewilderment and tears when things went badly for her, that he spoke to one of his professors at Dartmouth about her. After a visit to the Bridgman house, James Barrett's professor had an idea. In 1829, the very year of Laura's birth, the first school for the blind in the United States had been founded in Boston, Massachusetts. Its director, Dr. Samuel Gridley Howe, was especially interested in trying to educate the blind deaf, and Laura, with her eagerness for learning, seemed just the right person.

Sadly, this meant that Laura had to leave her home in New Hampshire and go to live at the school in Boston. She was not quite eight years old, and there was no way to explain gently to her that the life she'd known was ending and a new one was about to begin.

For the first few days Laura raged like a wounded animal and cried herself to sleep with exhaustion. But Dr. Howe and his sister, and the forty or so blind children and their teachers, soon became her second family. Even more wonderful was Dr. Howe's method of teaching Laura the names of things, starting with a key, a spoon, and other familiar objects. He would add a label to the object, with its name written in raised lettering for her to feel. This was before the braille system of writing for the blind, by means of raised dots, had come into general use.

Soon Laura learned the twenty-six letters of the alphabet and how to arrange them into words of all kinds, not just the names of objects. Laura also learned to "hear" by having the finger alphabet spelled into her hand and to "speak" to others by spelling the finger alphabet into theirs.

Although Laura made many visits to her family in New Hampshire, the Perkins Institution for the Blind in Boston remained her home for the rest of her life. She was taught arithmetic and geography, history and astronomy, read books from raised type, and wrote letters to her growing number of friends and admirers. She also did beautiful sewing and lacework and helped the teachers with the other blind students.

Laura Bridgman never learned to use her voice to speak fluently, but she pioneered the way for Helen Keller and other blind deaf children who would do that as well. Helen Keller's famous teacher, Anne Sullivan, was trained at Perkins, where she studied Dr. Howe's methods with Laura Bridgman.

In 1887, when Anne Sullivan went to Alabama to begin her work with six-year-old Helen Keller, she took along a doll that the grown Laura Bridgman had dressed and sent as a gift. A year later Helen was taken to Perkins to meet Laura Bridgman, the once terrified little girl from New Hampshire who had led the way in the flight from darkness and silence. Anne Sullivan's timing in bringing the two together was fortunate, for it was soon after—in 1889, in the sixtieth year of her life—that Laura Bridgman died.

# NEW JERSEY

New Jersey received its name in 1664 when Sir George Carteret, who had been governor of the Isle of Jersey in the English Channel, was given a land grant in America.

The coastal area was visited as early as 1524 by the Italian sea captain Giovanni da Verrazano. It was also explored in 1609 by Henry Hudson, who claimed it for the Dutch. The Indians of the region were an Algonquian people known to Europeans as the Delaware. However, they called themselves the Leni-Lenape, or "original people." Like neighboring New York, New Jersey was part of Dutch New Netherland until 1664, when it passed into English hands.

New Jersey was a major battleground during the American Revolution. It was the site of over a hundred clashes between the Continental Army and the British. New Jersey entered the Union, as the third state, on December 18, 1787.

Although heavily industrialized, New Jersey is known as *The Garden State* for its vegetable farms and fruit orchards. Other contrasting features are its sparsely inhabited marshy pinelands and its popular ocean beaches. Atlantic City, once a simple fishing village, became a fashionable resort in the late 1800s. But by 1930 it was shabby and neglected. A 1977 law permitting casino gambling brought new high-rise hotels and revived tourism.

**Question:** Who was "the Wizard of Menlo Park"?

**Answer:** Menlo Park is the name of what was once a small town in northeastern New Jersey. Its "wizard" was Thomas Alva Edison, who lived there from 1876 to 1886, working on some of his astonishing inventions such as the phonograph and the electric light.

168

# Atlantic City, Monopoly's Hometown

*Boardwalk. Park Place. Go to Jail. Pass Go, Collect $200.* If you've ever played Monopoly, which is said to be the world's most popular copyrighted board game, the above words are familiar to you. Boardwalk and all the streets are *real* place names in Atlantic City, New Jersey. Ventnor Avenue, Baltic Avenue, Marvin Gardens (even though the correct spelling is Marven Gardens) actually exist. How did this come about?

It all began in the Depression year of 1933. Ever since the stock-market crash of 1929, businesses had been failing and people were losing their jobs. Forty-four-year-old Charles G. Darrow, of the Germantown section of Philadelphia, found himself among the millions of unemployed. But Darrow's mind was buzzing with ideas and his dreams were very much alive.

In the days when he was more prosperous, Charles Darrow had often vacationed in Atlantic City, which had started to be developed in the 1850s. As the town was located on an island known as Absecon Beach, the first railroad line had to reach it via a causeway from the New Jersey mainland. Soon a six-hundred-room luxury hotel, the largest in the country, had been built. By the time Darrow was born, in 1889, the famous Boardwalk was lined with elegant hotels and shops, and a large amusement pier jutted out into the ocean. Now, though, in the 1930s, the "Queen of Resorts" had fallen on hard times, just like Darrow himself.

Few visitors rented the rolling chairs on which sightseers had once traveled the broad, five-mile-long, oceanfront Boardwalk. The merry-go-rounds and fortune-tellers' booths weren't doing a very good business. And even Atlantic City's famous saltwater taffy (not *really* made with salt water) wasn't selling very fast.

Darrow, though, managed to think in more optimistic terms. He saw poor, rundown Atlantic City as it once was—and as it might become again. Its properties would rise in value, vacationers would flock to it, and smart investors would be able to make a fortune in Atlantic City real estate. Soon Darrow was hard at work devising a board game for two to eight players. The object would be to buy, sell, rent, and trade various Atlantic City properties until one player owned the whole board.

Since he couldn't afford to have the game manufactured, Darrow made all the parts by hand—the playing boards, the cards, the play money, even the little green houses. He thought his idea was a pretty good one. So in 1934 he took his game to Parker Brothers, a large manufacturer and distributor of recreational items, to try to sell it. The Parker game experts conducted a "play test," went into conference, and reported back to Darrow. They told him that the game took too long to play and the rules were too complicated. All in all, it had "52 fundamental playing errors." In short, they felt that Darrow's real-estate game had no future.

Darrow was discouraged, but he didn't give up. He went on making the sets by hand and selling them on his own. Somehow people wanted them. Perhaps it was because *playing* at becoming a millionaire was the perfect pastime for people who'd been hit hard by the Depression.

In any case, Parker Brothers kept an eye on how surprisingly well Darrow was doing with his handmade sets, even though his profits were very small. And in 1935 they reconsidered and bought the rights. The game's name, Monopoly, became a registered trademark of the company. Soon Parker Brothers was making and selling twenty thousand sets a week, and they had a bonanza Christmas. But Parker saw Monopoly as a game for adults, and the company was so sure it would be a passing fad that it cut back production in 1936.

It was wrong! After a slight leveling-off, sales began to skyrocket.

Parents had taught the game to their children, and now entire families were playing it. Also, children proved that they were perfectly smart enough to master the "complicated" rules and to play it among themselves.

Today, over 100 million Monopoly sets have been sold in more than eighty countries around the world, and the game has been translated into at least twenty-three languages. In countries such as Britain, France, Spain, Germany, Israel, and others, the properties to be bought, sold, or traded are named after streets in their major cities. For example, London's Mayfair and Paris's rue de la Paix take the place of Atlantic City's Boardwalk.

In countries abroad, the game is also most often played with local currency, such as pesos in Mexico, rupees in India, and drachmas in Greece. Japan, however, is an exception. Though it uses Tokyo street names for its properties, it plays Monopoly with American dollars!

Monopoly has lent itself, too, to all sorts of contests and stunt events. Games have been played in tree houses, in elevators, on balance beams, in bathtubs, and even underwater, each vying for a world's record as the longest-running game in its category.

As of 1989, the *longest* game played anywhere was held at a McDonald's Restaurant in Bluffton, Ohio. It lasted for seventy days straight. The *largest* Monopoly game ever played took place on a "game board" that was the size of an entire city block, and the *smallest* Monopoly game is said to be one inch square. There are also Monopoly games in braille for players with visual handicaps.

As to the unemployed Charles G. Darrow—whatever happened to him? After Parker Brothers bought Monopoly and the game took off on a mass-marketed basis, all his dreams came true. At the age of forty-six he found himself a millionaire, and he never had to work again. Until his death in 1967, he traveled the world and devoted much of his time to collecting rare species of orchids.

Atlantic City's fortunes changed too, especially after 1977, when legal casino gambling was introduced. The old hotels were demolished with the wrecker's ball or blown up, and sleek new ones, with gambling and entertainment facilities, were erected. Although there *are* more jobs to be had in Monopoly's hometown than in the dark days of the 1930s, Atlantic City still has large pockets of poverty in the streets behind the flashy Boardwalk hotels.

# NEW MEXICO

CAPITAL: SANTA FE

New Mexico got its name from "old" Mexico, the country to its south. Mexico itself is named after the war god of the Aztec Indians, Mexitli. The New Mexico region was inhabited by Indian peoples as early as twelve thousand years ago. When Spanish explorers arrived from Mexico in the 1500s, they found Indian groups that farmed the land, made pottery and cloth, and lived in communities that resembled small cities. They gave them the name Pueblo, which is Spanish for "town."

Santa Fe, the oldest capital city in the United States, was founded by the Spanish in 1610, ten years before the Pilgrims landed at Plymouth Rock! It wasn't until the early 1800s that American trappers reached the area. Traders also appeared, bringing goods from the East along the newly opened Santa Fe Trail. Most of the New Mexico Territory was ceded to the United States at the end of the Mexican War, in 1848. New Mexico became a state of the Union on January 6, 1912. Nicknamed *The Land of Enchantment,* New Mexico is not only a blend of peoples— Native American, Hispanic, and Anglo—it also has a dramatically varied landscape, which includes twelve-thousand-foot forested mountains in the north and the eight-hundred-foot-deep fantastical world of Carlsbad Caverns in the south.

174

New Mexico has the largest uranium reserves in the United States. The sunny climate, Indian heritage, and popular arts and crafts of New Mexico attract many visitors.

> **Question**: Which state has a town named Truth or Consequences, after the popular radio show of the 1950s?
> **Answer**: New Mexico. In 1950, after playing host to a live broadcast of the show, Hot Springs, New Mexico, changed its name to Truth or Consequences. To its six thousand residents, it's known as *T* or *C.*

# Sky City, Home of the Acoma

"[We] found a [very high] rock with a village on top. It is one of the strongest places we have seen . . . with a rough ascent, so that we repented having climbed up to the top."

These words were written by Hernando de Alvarado, a member of the expedition led by Francisco Coronado into what is now the southwestern United States, in the year 1540. Coronado was traveling north from Mexico in search of the fabled Seven Cities of Cibola, said to be rich in gold, emeralds, and other jewels. But he and other wealth-seeking Spaniards were to find that no such cities existed.

Instead, Coronado and his men came upon a number of Indian villages perched on steep-sided, flat-topped hills known as mesas, which rose up from the high plains of the region. *Mesa* is the Spanish word for "table."

Why were the Indian peoples living atop these abrupt outcroppings of rock instead of on the plains below, where they cultivated their fields of corn, beans, squash, and cotton, and raised their flocks of turkeys? The answer was for purposes of defense. Long before the Spanish conquerors appeared, there had been repeated raids by Apaches, Comanches, and other Indian hunting peoples who grew no crops of their own.

In their high rock fortresses, the farming Indians kept well-filled granaries and supplies of water that could outlast a long siege, for even a year if necessary. But attempts at plunder seldom lasted very long. The cliff sides were difficult to scale because the ladders hidden in the rocky clefts were quickly hauled up. At the same time, stones and boulders were hurled down onto the enemy below.

The "Sky City" sighted by the Coronado expedition was one of the tallest. The mesa rose nearly four hundred feet above the high plain, so that those living on top were about seven thousand feet above sea level. Its people, numbering about six thousand, were called the Acoma, or Akomé, meaning "people of the white rock."

Their history contained many legends. One told of their having once lived on an even higher mesa known as Katzimo a short distance to the northeast. One day, when almost all the cliff dwellers were down on the plain below, harvesting their fields, a violent rainstorm burst forth. The torrent lasted for three days. The fields were flooded. But far worse, the rain had caused severe landslides, destroying the ladders and erasing the toeholds and fingerholds that had been used for scaling the walls of the mesa.

After the rains subsided, the harvesters anxiously began to circle the base of Katzimo. For days they listened to the weakening cries of those stranded in the village above, for most were either very elderly or very young. But the Acoma could find no way to return to the top of Katzimo. At last, having lost all hope of being reunited with their loved ones below, an old woman and her granddaughter leaped from the cliff to their death. It was then that the Acoma decided to abandon the cruel "Enchanted Mesa" of Katzimo.

The Acoma are believed to have built their new Sky City around 1150, if not earlier. Again, they constructed secret, twisting trails to the top, bringing up earth in buffalo-hide bags to build their adobe, or mud-brick, houses. There was no soil at all atop the bare-surfaced mesa, so earth for burying the dead also had to be hauled up, as did wood for fuel. Sky City houses were built two to three stories high. Usually the first level was a storehouse, containing dried foodstuffs, cotton for spinning and weaving cloth, and clay for pottery making. The second and third stories, reached directly by ladders or very steep, narrow steps, were the family's living quarters. Nearby were large, outdoor, beehive-shaped ovens for cooking and baking.

Survival atop the new mesa was made easier by the fact that its surface contained several rock pools that collected rainwater and melted snow. The Acoma were careful to keep their reservoirs free of pollution. Water was also brought to the village from streams and springs below. It was carried in large clay water jars, balanced on the heads of the Acoma. The Coronado expedition of 1540 did not attempt to conquer the Acoma.

But word of this and other prosperous farming pueblos got back to Mexico and Spain, and in December 1598 Juan de Zaldivar arrived with thirty-one men, demanding cornmeal for his party. Of those who attempted to scale the mesa, thirteen were killed, including Zaldivar. Now the Spanish felt they must severely punish the Acoma. In January 1599 a new force of seventy men was sent, under Zaldivar's brother Vicente.

This time the invaders reached the summit, burned the town, killed hundreds, tossed bodies over the cliffs, and took numerous prisoners—men, women, and children—whom they marched away to become laborers for the Spanish conquerors. All Acoma men over the age of twenty-five were treated with exceptional cruelty. They had one foot cut off to prevent their escape. We know all this because it was reported in the writings of the Spanish soldier-adventurer Gaspar Perez de Villagrá, which were published in Spain in 1610.

Amazingly, Sky City survived under the Spanish yoke. The Acoma were made to give up their own religion and help build a church atop the mesa, hauling earth, rocks, and huge logs on their backs, or leading pack animals up the new burro trail they had been forced to build. An Acoma revolt in 1680 sent the Spanish fleeing. But they returned in the 1690s, offering the Acoma horses, cattle, and sheep. These valuable animals had been unknown in America before the Spanish conquest.

When the New Mexico Territory was ceded to the United States in 1848, the land title of the Acoma to their Sky City was recognized by the new government. Today about fifteen hundred Acoma live in a well-kept village atop the mesa, some sixty-five miles west of Albuquerque. Having adopted almost no modern conveniences, they follow a way of life similar to that of their ancestors of nearly a thousand years ago, making Sky City probably the oldest continuously inhabited community in the United States.

Other Acoma have moved about eleven miles away, to Acomita, a government housing project near the railroad and the interstate highway, where they have electricity and running water, refrigerators and stoves, TV sets, supermarkets, and gas stations. Yet some Acoma live part of the time in *both* places, making a special point of returning to Sky City for the many festivals that are held there in celebration of their still richly alive past.

# NEW YORK

The Duke of York, brother of King Charles II of England, gave New York its name in 1664. Earlier it had been under Dutch rule and was known as New Netherland. Like New Jersey, the area was visited by Giovanni da Verrazano in 1524 and by Henry Hudson in 1609. Hudson, an Englishman sailing for the Dutch, explored the Hudson River all the way to the site of Albany. The Algonquian and the Iroquois, two major groups of Indian peoples, inhabited the region.

New York's nickname, *The Empire State,* can be traced to the years 1785 to 1790, when Congress met in New York City. While traveling in New York State shortly after the American Revolution, George Washington remarked that he saw it as "the seat of Empire." Statehood for New York came on July 26, 1788.

Parts of rural New York State are still noted for their agriculture, dairy products, and vineyards, while New York City is a major metropolis, a center of business, finance, and the arts. It has also been a great port of entry for immigrants. Nearly half the people in the United States today—around 100 million— can trace their ancestry to someone who came through Ellis Island between the 1890s and the 1920s. Important tourist sights in New York State include the Statue of Liberty and Niagara Falls.

179

**Question**: Are there really a Thousand Islands in the St. Lawrence River, on New York State's northern border with Canada?

**Answer**: Yes. In fact, there are said to be 1,753, give or take a few. Slightly more than half belong to Canada. Some are just mounds of rock and foliage. Others are four to five miles long and may contain a campsite, a summer home, or even a large stone mansion.

# Yours till Niagara Falls

"The Waters which fall from this horrible Precipice do foam and boyl after the most hideous manner imaginable." These words were written in 1678 by Father Louis Hennepin, a French missionary who was one of the first Europeans to see the crashing falls that the Indians called *Niagara*, or "thunderer."

Father Hennepin made a sketch of the area and took a guess that the height of the waters was about six hundred feet. Actually, the cascades of water at Niagara drop less than two hundred feet from their stone ridges into the river below. But their majesty and volume, their abrupt descent and exceptional width, make them a spectacular and even terrifying sight.

Starting in the early 1800s, Niagara Falls became a popular honeymoon destination. Possibly this all began when the nephew of the French emperor Napoleon Bonaparte visited with his bride in 1803. In any case, newly married couples from near and far were soon flocking to the spot where western New York State meets the Canadian province of Ontario.

The Falls themselves are located on an otherwise quiet stream, the Niagara River, which is only about thirty-five miles long. The waters of the Great Lakes empty out of Lake Erie and pass through the river on their way to Lake Ontario. But suddenly, about midway, they drop into a steep gorge, creating two major falls areas—the horseshoe-shaped Canadian Falls (over two thousand feet wide) and the straighter-shaped American Falls (over one thousand feet wide).

The Falls are believed to have been formed about twelve thousand years ago. Because of their great age and their never-ending flow of water, they appear to be the perfect symbol of permanence and faithfulness. So aside from being a delightful summer vacation spot following a June wedding, Niagara seems to promise a long and happy marriage. As the local saying goes, "The love of those who honeymoon here will last as long as the Falls themselves."

A shortened version, "Yours till Niagara Falls," has become more than just a pledge for newlyweds. Vacationers have written it on post-cards, friends have used it to sign off letters, and classmates have scrawled it in school yearbooks.

But how really long lived or permanent are the Falls at Niagara? Yosemite Falls in California is not only over two thousand feet higher than Niagara. It is millions of years older. Niagara is also a "moving" falls. Twelve thousand years ago, the Falls were seven miles north of where they are today. Each year, the rushing waters eat away at the rocky crests over which they flow. So in addition to moving slowly upstream on the Niagara River, the Falls are gradually becoming lower. Scientists estimate that in about 130,000 years the Falls may actually be reduced to a series of white-water rapids near the present-day site of the city of Buffalo!

Meantime, though—and probably for the next 2,500 years—Niagara Falls should look much as it has since the days of Father Hennepin, except of course for its tourist facilities and its hydroelectric power plant. As much as three-fourths of the water that flows through the Niagara River is drawn off to generate electricity before it reaches the Falls. Most of the siphoning is done at night and out of season so that fair-weather visitors will see the Falls at their best.

Throughout the 1800s, Niagara Falls drew sightseers of renown. They included Queen Victoria of England, the famed British author Charles Dickens, and the Civil War hero who was to become United States president, General Ulysses S. Grant. Another visitor of note was the young Helen Keller, the blind and deaf girl who had learned to speak and write. In March 1893, at the age of twelve and a half, Helen visited the Falls. Their power was so great that it was able to penetrate the dark and silent world in which she lived. Helen Keller wrote that she "stood on the point which overhangs the American Falls and felt the air vibrate and the earth tremble."

Just as some people today will dive off high bridges or walk a tight-rope between two tall buildings, there were those who couldn't resist risking their lives in daredevil stunts at Niagara Falls.

In 1829, a Rhode Islander named Sam Patch dove a hundred feet into the swirling waters just below the Falls. He jumped from a plat-form on Goat Island in the middle of the Niagara River. Sam Patch survived two dives at Niagara but lost his life the third time around, when he tried a similar feat at another waterfall in New York State.

Thirty years later, in 1859 and 1860, a French tightrope walker,

Jean-François Gravelet, did a series of thrilling stunts, inching his way on a high wire stretched from the American to the Canadian side of the Falls. Gravelet, who went by the stage name of "The Great Blondin," not only *walked* across the rope above the churning waters. He sat down, he turned somersaults, he stood on a chair balanced on the rope. He even made the crossing carrying his manager on his back! He also managed to die in bed in his seventies.

Not to be outdone, in 1901 a Michigan schoolteacher, Annie Edson Taylor, decided to try going over the American Falls strapped into a large, padded barrel. Mrs. Taylor, who couldn't even swim, was sealed into her barrel and sent crashing down the wall of water. Fortunately, the barrel bobbed over to the Canadian side and was able to be pulled ashore. When the barrel was opened, Mrs. Taylor had a gash in her head and a startled expression on her face. She wanted to know if she'd gone over the Falls yet!

Although Annie Edson Taylor didn't care to repeat her experience, others did, in spite of the fact that all such stunts were declared illegal in 1912. One of the greatest hazards was the whirlpool at the base of the Falls that waited to suck one under. Between the 1920s and the 1950s, several barrelers lost their lives, while others who survived were immediately arrested.

Freak accidents, too, have claimed lives at powerful Niagara. But there have also been rescues and lucky survivals. In 1960, two children and an adult were sailing in a small boat on the Niagara River, not realizing how close they were to the Falls area. Before they could change course, they found themselves being rushed toward the crest of the Horseshoe Falls. The older child, a girl, was grabbed from the boat as it slid past Goat Island. But the younger child, a seven-year-old boy named Roger Woodward, and the older person were dashed over the Falls.

The grown-up did not survive. But miraculously young Roger did. He escaped being caught in the dread rapids of the whirlpool, and was rescued by a sight-seeing boat farther downstream. Niagara Falls had proved once again that nature can be cruel and kind by turns. Father Hennepin was surely right when, marveling at the might of its waters, he wrote, "The Universe does not afford its Parallel."

# NORTH CAROLINA

CAPITAL: RALEIGH

In the early 1600s, the territory of both North and South Carolina was known as Carolana. It was named for King Charles I of England. "Carolana" comes from *Carolus,* the Latin for Charles. Charles II changed the spelling to Carolina, and in the early 1700s the region was separated into provinces known as North Carolina and South Carolina. From the time it was granted statehood, on November 21, 1789, North Carolina has been called *The Old North State.*

The coastal region was explored by the French and the Spanish in the early 1500s. But it was the English who tried to settle colonists on Roanoke Island, just off the coast, in 1585 and again in 1587. Their efforts to plant a permanent colony failed due to the mysterious disappearance of what became known as the Lost Colony.

*The Tar Heel State,* another nickname, comes from Civil War days, when a proud and stubborn North Carolina regiment is said to have dug in its heels on the battlefield—just as if they were stuck in tar. North Carolina's coastal island chain, known as the Outer Banks, was the site in 1903 of Orville and Wilbur Wright's first successful flight of a power-driven airplane. The low-lying sandy dunes of eastern North Carolina give way to a terrain that rises gradually toward the Blue Ridge Mountains in the western part of the state.

**Question:** Which state has the highest mountain east of the Mississippi?
**Answer:** North Carolina. Mount Mitchell (6,684 feet) is the highest point in the eastern United States.

# Was the "Lost Colony" Really Lost?

What must it have been like to be among the first English children to sail for America, in the year 1587? Never before had entire families—mothers, fathers, and children—taken ship for the New World to plant a colony. Two years earlier, in 1585, a company of 108 men had tried to start a settlement in the vast new territory that Queen Elizabeth had granted to Sir Walter Raleigh. They had chosen a bit of land called Roanoke Island. It lay between the mainland and an outer chain of islands, in what would one day be known as North Carolina. At the time, though, the entire territory was called Virginia, after Elizabeth, the Virgin Queen.

It was true that the 1585 expedition had not been a success, for 103 of the men who had intended to start the settlement had returned to England the following year. Foolishly, they had made enemies of the island's friendly Algonquian inhabitants. They had actually killed and beheaded the Indians' chief.

This time, though, everything was going to be different. Instead of an assortment of adventuring men who were more interested in immediate wealth than in planting a colony, there would be fourteen middle-class families among the 117 colonists.

The governor would be John White, an experienced member of the 1585 expedition who was also an artist and had brought back many paintings and drawings of the land and its people. And wisely, the new colonists would not attempt to land on Roanoke Island, where the local Indians were sure to have bad memories of their countrymen. They would sail a bit farther north and make their colony on the shore of Chesapeake Bay.

On May 8, 1587, the small fleet of ships carrying eighty-nine men, seventeen women, and eleven children set sail. Among the passengers was John White's daughter, Eleanor, and her husband, Ananias Dare. Eleanor was already pregnant with her first child. But she chose to brave the unknown in the company of her husband and her father.

As on the 1585 voyage, the ships took a southerly route, stopping at islands in the Caribbean to gather live samples of pineapple and banana plants, which the settlers hoped to grow in their new colony. The children had an especially wonderful time as they disembarked at Saint Croix in the Virgin Islands. Never before had they romped about in such balmy warmth, seen such rich foliage and colorful flowers, or heard the screams of tropical birds. Innocently they picked and ate "a small fruite like greene apples." But at once they cried out in pain as their mouths burned and their tongues swelled and blistered. For this was the wild-growing manchineel, the poisonous fruit of a deadly tropical tree.

Happily no deaths were reported. But this episode may have been an omen of a much more serious mistake to come. On July 22 the fleet reached Roanoke Island to check on the abandoned fort and dwelling huts of the 1585 settlers. As feared, the handful of men left behind to hold the fort had vanished. But the huts themselves were still standing, overgrown with pumpkin vines on which deer were feeding. To the surprise of the colonists, the captain of the fleet suddenly ordered everyone ashore. His excuse was that it was too late in the summer to risk the gales and hurricanes of August seeking an unknown destination on the shore of Chesapeake Bay.

Given no choice, the colonists soon set about repairing the old huts and building new ones. The women set up housekeeping, and the children had a fine time fishing and catching the delicious blue crabs of the local waters. But it *was* too late in the summer for planting and, after a month of trying not too successfully to patch things up with the local Indians, John White realized that he would have to return to England for supplies. On August 18 his daughter gave birth to a little girl, the first English child born on American soil. She was christened Virginia, after the name of the territory. Nine days later, on August 27, John White sailed for England and help.

As history tells us, he never saw his daughter, his grandchild, or any member of the colony again. War between England and Spain delayed his return to Roanoke for three years. When at last he reached the island in August of 1590, it was deserted. The only message was the word CROATOAN carved on a post at the entrance to the abandoned fort and huts.

White did not lose all hope, however. He had expected that the colonists might at some point move south to the island then known as Croatoan, near Cape Hattaras. Croatoan Island was the home of the Indian Manteo, with whom the English had made friends on the 1585 journey, and who had actually visited England.

White's search seemed almost over. He directed the captain to sail south to Croatoan Island. But this was not to be. Once again it was hurricane season in these waters, and the ship was rapidly blown off course. White returned to England, and for reasons unknown, no further searches were made.

To this day, no one knows for sure what happened to the Lost Colony. Among the theories are death from starvation or disease, or from Spanish swords or Indian arrows. As recently as the 1930s a series of stones engraved with bleak and dire messages from Eleanor Dare to her father, John White, began to turn up. All, however, were proved to be fakes. They included words that were not yet in use in the English language in the late 1500s!

Most believable, and happiest, is the possibility that the colonists did indeed join Manteo and his people on Croatoan Island. Around 1650 members of this Indian group are known to have moved to the mainland. Among them were blue-eyed and fair-haired individuals.

Today their descendants live mainly in Robeson County in southeastern North Carolina, and among them can be found the family names of forty-one members of the Lost Colony. So perhaps the children of 1587 had a pleasant and fruitful life after all. Perhaps the Lost Colony wasn't truly lost. It was only John White and those who never found it who were.

# NORTH DAKOTA

CAPITAL: BISMARCK

A Sioux Indian people who called themselves the Dakota gave North Dakota its name. The word *Dakota* meant "friends," or "allies." The region was Indian buffalo-hunting country when it was first explored by a French-Canadian trader and trapper in 1738. With the Louisiana Purchase of 1803, most of the North Dakota territory came under the control of the United States. In the early 1800s the Lewis and Clark Expedition wintered in the region on its way to the Pacific Coast.

North Dakota is nicknamed *The Flickertail State* because of the many flickertail ground squirrels that inhabited its rugged prairie-lands. Settlement of these northern plains was slow until the late 1800s, when huge tracts of cropland known as bonanza farms were developed for wheat growing. North Dakota was admitted to the Union on November 2, 1889.

Today North Dakota is still a leading producer of wheat, most of it grown on highly mechanized farms. Livestock are raised on lands where the buffalo once roamed. And manufacturing, as well as oil and gas production, has become part of North Dakota's economy.

---

**Question**: What was the Great Dakota Mystery?

**Answer**: As President Benjamin Harrison was about to sign the proclamations for the two newly admitted states of North Dakota and South Dakota, on November 2, 1889, he deliberately shuffled the papers. So as not to appear to show any favoritism, he didn't want to know which one he was signing first. Officially, though, North Dakota is ranked thirty-ninth to enter the Union and South Dakota fortieth, in alphabetical order.

---

# Sacagawea, a Gift from the Plains

In North Dakota they have a saying: "If you don't like the weather, just wait a minute." For in this state—which lies at the geographical center of the North American continent—sudden and extreme climate changes are no surprise. Even in May the winds can howl and snow can fall.

Yet from October of 1804 to April of 1805, the Lewis and Clark Expedition wintered among the Mandan and Hidatsa Indian peoples of present-day North Dakota. This was the longest stopover the party made on its more than two-year, nearly eight-thousand-mile trek from the Mississippi River to the Pacific Ocean and back.

The purposes of the trailblazing journey were many. Even before the Louisiana Purchase of 1803, President Thomas Jefferson had been eager for the American continent, much of it still in foreign hands, to be explored to its western shore. He was interested, too, in finding a direct route to the Far East, in developing the fur trade, and in learning more about the continent's Native American inhabitants. Experienced soldiers and frontiersmen, Meriwether Lewis and William Clark were also charged with making a scientific study of the many unfamiliar varieties of plants and animals that they would encounter.

LEWIS

CLARK

The winter camp, known as Fort Mandan, was built overlooking the Missouri River, north of the present site of Bismarck, North Dakota. The Mandans were a crop-growing people who exchanged their corn, beans, squash, and tobacco with other Indians and with white traders for meats and hides. Despite howling blizzards and fifty-below-zero temperatures, they visited the fort often to examine the tools, weapons, and other possessions of the forty-man "Corps of Discovery" from the East.

Among the visitors was a French-Canadian trapper, Toussaint Charbonneau, who lived among the local Indians and could translate their language. One of his two wives was a young woman of about sixteen named Sacagawea. She was a Shoshoni, whose people lived in the region that is today Montana and Idaho. But as a child of twelve or so, she had been captured by enemies of the Shoshoni and eventually brought to the Mandan and Hidatsa villages.

Soon it was agreed that when spring came, Charbonneau and Sacagawea would continue west with the expedition as guides and interpreters. Sacagawea would be especially helpful when they reached the Shoshoni country, for there Lewis and Clark hoped to buy horses to use as pack animals in crossing the mountains that lay ahead.

On February 11, 1805, Sacagawea gave birth to her first child, a little boy who was named Jean Baptiste but was nicknamed Pompey, or Pomp. This posed no problem for Sacagawea. When the party set out from Fort Mandan in April, she simply strapped little two-month-old Pomp to her back.

SHOSHONI VILLAGE

Baby or no, and the only woman in the party, Sacagawea soon proved to be a lot more helpful than her husband, Charbonneau. Not only did she find the best-eating roots and grasses to go with the plentiful game the party shot. She also proved quick thinking and brave when her excitable husband nearly sank one of the river canoes, which had been struck by a sudden gust of wind. Although Sacagawea (who could not swim) was nearly washed overboard with her baby, she remained calm and leaned far out over the water to try to save the journals, maps, medicines, and other supplies that were still afloat.

In August 1805 the expedition reached the Shoshoni camp of Chief Cameahwait in what is today Idaho. Called on to act as interpreter, Sacagawea went forward to speak to her own people. To her great joy and surprise, she discovered that the chief was her very own brother, from whom she had been parted several years earlier. But Cameahwait didn't seem to return her enthusiasm. Perhaps he was wary of her white companions. Sacagawea did, however, help the expedition bargain for the much-needed horses, and after a stay of two and a half weeks, the group set out on the perilous but successful journey across the mountains to the shores of the Pacific.

A year later, in August 1806, Sacagawea, Charbonneau, and Pomp were back among the Mandans. Charbonneau was paid for his and his wife's services, and the rest of the expedition continued eastward. Sacagawea had faced and overcome all the hardships of the journey with intelligence and liveliness. She had been especially delighted to reach the shore of the Pacific Ocean, in Oregon, where she saw the remains of a beached whale. Unlike her irritable and difficult husband, she would be missed by everyone. For Lewis and Clark, and the members of the Corps of Discovery, she had indeed been a gift of their inhospitable winter on the plains of North Dakota.

Little is known of Sacagawea's fate. Some say she lived into her nineties and died on a Shoshoni reservation in 1884. But most historians believe she died in 1812 of a fever, a few months after giving birth to a baby girl. She would have been about twenty-five years old. The fate of her son Pomp is also uncertain. He is believed to have been raised from about the age of five by William Clark, who had taken a great liking to the child. He may have become, like his mother, a guide and interpreter.

Sacagawea herself is remembered with plaques, monuments, and place names throughout the "Lewis and Clark country" that she traversed. And in North Dakota—where she first became known to history—she is honored with a statue placed on the grounds of the state capitol at Bismarck.

# OHIO

Ohio takes its name from an Iroquois Indian word meaning "big," or "great." The Indians first used this word to describe the Ohio River. The Ohio forms part of the eastern boundary and all of the southern boundary of the state, and flows eventually into the Mississippi. Lake Erie, one of the Great Lakes, makes up most of the state's northern boundary. These and other waterways have helped to make Ohio a leading industrial state.

Although first claimed by the French and then by the English, the Ohio region became part of the United States after the American Revolution. Ohio entered the Union on March 1, 1803, as the first state west of the Allegheny Mountains. Its nickname, *The Buckeye State,* comes from its native buckeye, or horse-chestnut, trees. Their large seeds are not the kind that are good to eat. They are called buckeyes because of brown markings on the shells that make them look a little like the eye of a buck, or deer.

**OHIO ENTERED THE UNION AS THE 17TH STATE**

Because of its long river border with the slaveholding state of Kentucky, Ohio played an important role in helping runaway slaves go north in pre–Civil War days. The network that helped fugitives flee toward Canada and safety was known as the Underground Railroad.

---

**Question**: Here's a riddle about a state, which poses the question: What's round at both ends and high in the middle?
**Answer**: O-HI-O.

---

195

# Heading North on the Underground Railroad

The Underground Railroad wasn't a real railroad. It had no tracks, no locomotives, and no railway cars. Yet it had "conductors" and "stationmasters," "waiting rooms" and "depots." And to be "catching the next train" meant something very special. It meant that an escaped slave from the American South was heading north toward freedom.

The Underground Railroad started "running" some time around 1830. It even had a "president" who was secretly known to the conductors. His name was Levi Coffin.

LEVI COFFIN

Like William Penn, the founder of the colony of Pennsylvania, Levi Coffin was a Quaker, a member of the Society of Friends. This religious group, which opposed violence in all forms, was against slavery. Coffin, who was born in the late 1700s, lived for a time in North Carolina. He had witnessed the rapid growth of slave labor in the cotton fields of the South after 1793, when Eli Whitney's invention of the cotton gin made cotton growing increasingly profitable. After helping a number of ill-treated slaves escape, Coffin himself moved north and finally settled in Cincinnati, Ohio. It was a group of bitter Southern slaveholders who first dubbed him "president of the Underground Railroad."

There were several routes by which a runaway slave could escape to the North. The route from slaveholding Kentucky to slave-free Ohio was among the most used because the two states were separated by the Ohio River, parts of which froze in winter. Fleeing slaves could then cross the river by foot on the ice. Once ashore in Ohio, there were "stations" close to the river where fugitives could be safely hidden until transportation farther north could be arranged.

There were numerous ways of smuggling the escaped slaves from one Underground Railroad "stop" to another. Often they were driven in wagons under loads of straw or other goods. Some were transported in hearses as make-believe corpses. Others rode boldly in view, dressed in widows' clothing and wearing heavy black veils. At the stations where they transferred to some other conductor, the escapees might be hidden in cupboards, behind specially built false walls, in old trunks in attics, in corncribs or barns. One Ohio stationmaster dug a tunnel from his house to his barn where runaways could hide without being found in either place.

One of the most active stations on the Ohio riverfront was the home of the Reverend John Rankin, in the town of Ripley. It was to Rankin's house one day that a young black woman carrying a child appeared seeking refuge. She was drenched and exhausted, and was shivering with cold, for the ice on the river had started to break up, and many times she had sunken to her waist as she struggled from one floating cake of ice to another.

The story of the young woman reached the ears of Harriet Beecher Stowe, who would later become famous as the author of the antislavery novel *Uncle Tom's Cabin*. Between 1832 and 1850 Mrs. Stowe and her family lived in Cincinnati, where she heard many harrowing tales of slave escapes. When *Uncle Tom's Cabin* first appeared in print in 1851, one of the most dramatic scenes was that of Eliza crossing the ice with slave catchers at her heels. Mrs. Stowe described how, with her child in her arms, Eliza leaped onto the first of many rafts of ice, struggling "with wild cries and desperate energy . . . till dimly, as in a dream, she saw the Ohio side, and a man helping her up the bank."

Unfortunately, simply passing from a slaveholding state to a nonslave state was not a complete guarantee of safety for a black person. Just as there were some six million whites in the South who did not hold slaves (and many Southerners who opposed slavery), there were also many people in the North who supported slavery. This became especially clear after the passage of the Fugitive Slave Law of 1850. This law allowed any white person to accuse a black person of being a runaway slave without proof of identification. The accused was not allowed self-defense or a trial by jury. A local judge would decide the case. If the judge returned the accused to slavery, the judge received ten dollars. If he let the accused go free, the judge got only five dollars!

The operators of the Underground Railroad knew that this law was aimed largely at them, because of the tens of thousands of slaves they had already helped toward freedom. Between 1850 and the outbreak of the Civil War in 1861, the railroad increased its efforts to transport slaves both out of the South *and* out of the country—to Canada and even to England. It was estimated that, all together, over a hundred thousand runaways became free persons by means of the Underground Railroad.

One famous escapee to Canada was Josiah Henson, who had been a slave in Maryland and seen numerous hardships, about which he wrote in his autobiography, published in 1849. Some of the harsh experiences of Harriet Beecher Stowe's Uncle Tom were drawn from the life of Josiah Henson. But Uncle Tom, the unresisting, obedient slave—who later came to be despised by blacks for his long-suffering ways—was in no other way similar to Josiah Henson. Henson founded

JOSIAH HENSON

a school for black fugitives in Canada, lectured widely, and was received by Queen Victoria on a visit to England after the Civil War.

However, the picture that Harriet Beecher Stowe drew by keeping her fictional Uncle Tom *in* slavery was enormously effective in promoting antislavery feelings throughout the country. In 1862, while the Civil War was raging, Mrs. Stowe went to Washington to meet President Abraham Lincoln. He is reported to have greeted her with the words, "Ah, so you are the little lady who wrote the book that made this big war!"

Perhaps that was an exaggeration. Yet there was no question that Harriet Beecher Stowe's years in Ohio, among the people of the Underground Railroad, gave her deep insights into slave life. Her sense of outrage would affect an entire nation and an entire people.

# OKLAHOMA

Oklahoma, or "land of the red people," comes from the Choctaw Indian words *okla* (people) and *homa* (red). The Choctaws, along with the Cherokee, Creek, Chickasaw, and Seminole Indians, were latecomers to the Oklahoma region. They lived originally in the Southeast. As their lands were taken by white settlers, they were forced, between 1820 and 1846, to resettle in this western reserve, known then as Indian Territory.

Gold-seeking Spanish explorers first reached this region in the 1500s. It was at that time inhabited mainly by buffalo-hunting Indians. Later it was claimed by the French. Most of the Oklahoma territory passed into American hands through the Louisiana Purchase of 1803.

Oklahoma's nickname *The Sooner State* comes from the land rushes of 1889 and 1893, when the Indians' promised preserve was opened to white settlement by the government. Those who jumped the official signal for staking out land claims were known as sooners. Another nickname, *The Boomer State,* comes from an organized group called the Boomers who agitated for the use of the rich cattle-grazing lands in the Indian Territory.

Statehood for Oklahoma came on November 16, 1907. The discovery of oil brought great wealth to the state. But the careless use of its agricultural lands also led to the dust-bowl years of the 1930s, when starving "Okies" were driven from their homes by a severe drought. Today Oklahoma's croplands are irrigated and better managed. Oil and natural gas are still produced, and aerospace and aviation industries have been developed.

---

**Question**: What is the Oklahoma panhandle?
**Answer**: Oklahoma is shaped like a very large, deep frying pan. The panhandle is the narrow strip of land in the western part of the state.

---

# Sooners and Boomers in Indian Territory

"As long as grass shall grow and rivers run . . ." These were the words of a United States government treaty guaranteeing the Indians of the Oklahoma territory that they would own their land in that western reserve forever.

This promise had been made during the first half of the 1800s, when the so-called Five Civilized Tribes—the Choctaw, Chickasaw, Cherokee, Creek, and Seminole—were forced to move out of Georgia, Florida, and other southeastern states to make way for white settlement. After their long trek westward, known as the Trail of Tears, the Indians pioneered the land and made a new life for themselves, protected from white intrusion.

But now, in 1889, the promise to the Indians was about to be broken. The lame excuse offered by the federal government was that the Indians had lost the right of sole residence in the region because some had fought on the side of the South during the Civil War. The truth, however, was that the western half of the country had been filling up with white homesteaders so rapidly that there was almost no place left to settle except in Oklahoma. By the 1870s a group of cattlemen called the Boomers started trying to move in on the Indians' grasslands. Others wanted land in the territory for wheat and cotton farming. And with the railroad coming through, there were those who saw the chance to grab property on which towns would be built.

April 22, 1889, was the day for the great free-for-all in the Oklahoma territory. All one had to do to be part of the land rush was to line up at one of the starting points and wait for the pistol shot or bugle blast that was set to go off at noon. Then the mad dash would begin. By covered wagon or fast-moving buggy, on the back of a mule or a mustang, and even on foot people raced for land. One man rode a steer and another was said to have been seen on the back of an ostrich!

As soon as a family found a likely spot, the next step was to jam sticks into the ground as boundaries and to set up a tent or other makeshift dwelling. Of course, fights broke out among the squatters. And worst of all, even the earliest arrivals often found that someone had gotten there before them. These were the "sooners." Some were officials, such as land-office men, soldiers, or marshals who took advantage of having the "inside track." Others were simply homestead seekers who'd managed to sneak across the line before the official hour.

To add to the greed and panic of the Oklahoma land grab, a number of railroad trains were slated to steam into the area shortly after noon on April 22. Their destination was the town site of

Guthrie, which consisted of nothing more than a water tank and a few shanties housing a station, a Wells Fargo depot, and a government land office.

The first train arrived at one thirty P.M. with people packed into the coaches and freight cars, others riding on the roofs and clinging to the sides. "I remember throwing my blankets out the car window the instant we stopped at the station," one lot seeker wrote. Then he tumbled "after them through the self-same window" and "joined the wild scramble for a town lot . . . without cost and without price." A very fat man wasn't so lucky. He also attempted to leave the train by the window but got stuck halfway through and yelled in vain for someone to rescue him.

By that evening Guthrie had become a tent city of over fifteen thousand people. And well over fifty thousand had staked claims throughout the region. A month later town lots, obtained free in

Guthrie, sold for two thousand dollars, and most of the tents had been replaced with wood or brick buildings. Supplies hauled in by train gave the town an electric-light plant, a waterworks, and banks, stores, and hotels as well.

At once a clamor went up for more land to be made available in Oklahoma. So additional areas were soon opened for settlement. The last of the big rushes, on a first-come, first-served basis, was into the Cherokee Strip, also called the Cherokee Outlet, in northern Oklahoma. It took place on September 16, 1893. This time the land seekers were lined up for fifty miles along the border waiting for the noon gun. And so desperate was the race that wagons crashed and riders were thrown, and those in the lead actually set fire to the grass to keep others from reaching the choicest lots.

Again there were sooners who'd gotten there before anybody else. Some were found sitting smugly in their wagons selling water to the panting newcomers for fifty cents a glass. Perhaps it was just as well that, before the day ended, an Oklahoma dust storm descended on the new encampment. The fighting over claims ceased as people withdrew into their tents and fastened down the flaps. Heated tempers cooled while the prairie wind blew for three whole days.

The violence of the 1893 land rush gave the federal authorities the idea that a lottery might be a better way to run things than a free-for-all. So for yet another Oklahoma land opening, in 1901, would-be homesteaders put their names in sealed envelopes. There were about 170,000 applicants for the 13,000 homesteads that were left. It took a month to complete the drawing, but the lottery worked. Another land rush might well have ended in a massacre.

By the time Oklahoma was ready for statehood, in 1907, the last large tracts of land, in what had once been Indian territory exclusively, had been settled. Some of the new home-steaders were black, but the vast majority were white. In fact, they outnumbered the Indians five to one. There was no question that the promise made to the Indians for "as long as grass shall grow and rivers run" had been broken.

# OREGON

CAPITAL: SALEM

Oregon may have taken its name from *ouragan,* the French word for "hurricane." Perhaps an early French traveler was caught in a fierce mountain or coastal storm, but no one is absolutely certain. The first European visitors to the region included Spanish and English sea captains sailing the Pacific Coast. In 1792 an American captain, Robert Gray, discovered and named the Columbia River. Lewis and Clark reached the mouth of the Columbia via their overland expedition in 1805. Among the Indians of the region were the Chinook, who lived by spearing the salmon that swam upstream each spring to lay their eggs.

Oregon's nickname, *The Beaver State,* comes from the vast trade in beaver skins carried on during the first half of the 1800s. Between the 1840s and the 1860s, many thousands of settlers traveled the two-thousand-mile Oregon Trail. It led from Independence, Missouri, to the "Oregon country," which then included Washington and Idaho, as well as parts of Montana and Wyoming. Following the settlement of British claims in the area, Oregon became a state of the Union, on February 14, 1859.

Oregon is today a leading lumbering and agricultural state. Most of its natural wealth comes from the moist, temperate sector that lies west of the Cascade Range. This mountain barrier prevents the warm sea winds of the Pacific from crossing into eastern Oregon, which has a drier climate, with colder winters and warmer summers.

---

**Question**: Where is the deepest lake in the United States?

**Answer**: In southwestern Oregon. Crater Lake, one of the world's scenic wonders, was created nearly seven thousand years ago when an ancient twelve-thousand-foot volcano, Mount Mazama, erupted. Its cone collapsed, leaving a huge bowl that eventually filled up with water nearly two thousand feet deep.

---

# "Dear Diary" on the Oregon Trail

"I begin to have some misgivings and fears. I shall be in a strange land without one friend." These were the words that eighteen-year-old Rebecca Ketcham confided to her diary in August of 1853 as she traveled west in a wagon train on the Oregon Trail. The party had started its overland journey of two thousand miles at Independence, in western Missouri. Almost all of its members had come an even longer way. Rebecca herself was from Ithaca, New York.

Like many long-distance travelers of her day, Rebecca kept a diary to record her experiences and, in her case, her innermost feelings. She needed a companion for her thoughts, for she was doing something rather unusual for her time. She was a young, unmarried woman who was traveling all on her own.

We never learn from Rebecca's diary *why* she had left her teaching post in New York State and made up her mind to cross the country in order to become a schoolteacher in Oregon. Was it a disagreement with her family, a broken love affair, a strong desire to see distant places?

In any case, Rebecca was given $240 by friends and relatives, and she started on her way. She traveled by stagecoach from Oswego,

New York, a town south of Ithaca, all the way to Missouri. Connections had to be made at various points along the route, in Pennsylvania, Ohio, and beyond, for no *one* stagecoach line covered the entire distance. This part of the journey, Rebecca wrote, cost her $34.58. Although she herself expressed wonder at how she "could have undertaken such an expedition," she was optimistic and in good spirits when she met her fellow travelers in Independence.

In addition to sharing the hardships and chores of the trail for five to six months, travelers had to pay the captain of the wagon train for leading them to their destination. Rebecca was charged $150 by Captain William Gray, who was to take the overland party across Nebraska, the Rockies, and the Cascades to the fertile Clatsop Plains region of northwestern Oregon. Although this payment left Rebecca with only about fifty-five dollars of her original stake, she expected she would be furnished with a mattress, a tent or wagon space for sleeping, food, and some other modest necessities. She understood, of course, that she had to help with the washing of clothes whenever the wagons reached a river or stream, even though the sun, wind, hard soap, and cold water left her arms "red and swollen and painful as though scalded with boiling water."

She helped too with gathering berries, herbs, and other wild foods, with collecting wood or dried buffalo chips for the cooking fires, and with hauling the water, milking the cows, and washing up the dishes, pots, and pans after meals.

But to her dismay, things weren't turning out as she'd expected. Instead of being given space in the wagons with the women, she was made to ride a tired old horse that often fell behind the wagon train, leaving her terrified that she would be forgotten and lost. Also, the summer of 1853 was exceptionally rainy. But even during a heavy rainstorm, she was not offered shelter in the wagons. Captain Gray simply gave her a rubber overcoat that covered only her "shoulders and arms and a very little of one side of [her] skirt." She was soon muddy and drenched, her "feet and limbs cold as ice."

Rebecca felt miserably slighted too by the sleeping and eating arrangements. No mattress was given her and she had to make do with a coarse blanket. At mealtimes the men in the party ate all the "stewed peaches" or "rice and apples . . . before [the] ladies had any." It wasn't unusual, of course, for women to provide the cooking, as well as the sewing, scrubbing, churning, and child caring, and to

BUFFALO COW AND CALF

be left with the poorest remains of the meal. Women made up only about one-seventh of the overland travelers—one woman to every six men—so their skills were in high demand.

In Rebecca's party the women seemed to be an especially disgruntled lot. Perhaps that was why they were unfriendly to Rebecca. Or were there other reasons? Did they feel that a young woman traveling alone wasn't suitable company for them and their young daughters?

Seldom invited to share their wagons and feeling out of place riding horseback with the men, Rebecca all but wept into her diary. She missed her mother and sister as she struggled through the days, "without a word of care or sympathy," feeling "so wronged, so illy treated."

Then one day it occurred to Rebecca to try to find out what some of the other members of the wagon train had paid Captain Gray. "I had the curiosity to ask James how much [the captain] charged him for taking him over." James was one of the unmarried young men in the party. The answer Rebecca received was a bit vague ... "from $50 to $100."

Anger rose up in Rebecca Ketcham as she realized that she'd been charged more than any other single member of the trail party. She could only assume that this was because she was a woman on her own, with no male relative to "protect" her. With fierce pride she wrote in her diary, "If that is the case, I don't work anymore. . . . Charge me $150," Rebecca added, "and then expect me to work my way. I think I shall find more time to write hereafter."

We don't know if Rebecca confronted Captain Gray, or simply reduced her work load on her own. But we're grateful that she did write in her diary more often after that, giving us lively descriptions of the journey itself and the surrounding country. Also, she made up her mind to ignore her small-minded and unfriendly companions and happily fulfilled her dream of getting to Oregon. There, just as she'd intended, Rebecca became a schoolteacher.

She had charge of a typical one-room schoolhouse made of rough-hewn logs, and she watched it fill up with the children of the wagon-train families that continued to arrive from the East.

Within two years of her arrival in Oregon, Rebecca Ketcham met and married a man named Finis E. Mills, a member of the board of trustees of the local Presbyterian Church. She had two sons. By that time Rebecca had stopped writing in her diary. Perhaps she felt that it had served its purpose in helping her overcome her fears and loneliness. For us, Rebecca Ketcham's diary serves another purpose. It tells us the story of a courageous young woman of the 1850s whose independent spirit broke new ground on the pioneer trail to Oregon.

SHE FELT SLIGHTED . . .

# PENNSYLVANIA

CAPITAL: HARRISBURG

"Pennsylvania" is another way of saying "Penn's Woods." King Charles II of England granted the land for the colony to William Penn in 1681, as payment of a debt owed to his father, Admiral Sir William Penn. "Sylvania" comes from the Latin *silvanus,* referring to forest or woods. The first European to reach the area is believed to have been Henry Hudson, in 1609. Indians of the Algonquian family lived there. Although Hudson claimed the territory for the Dutch, under whose flag he sailed, it passed into English hands in 1664.

WILLIAM PENN

Pennsylvania, *The Quaker State,* takes its nickname from the religious faith of William Penn, the younger. Penn had been persecuted in England as a Quaker, and he was determined that Pennsylvania should be a place where people of all faiths would have religious freedom. Another nickname, *The Keystone State,* refers to colonial Pennsylvania's central location among the Thirteen Colonies. Like the keystone of an arch, which serves to lock all the other stones into place, Pennsylvania appeared to hold the New England and Southern colonies together.

Pennsylvania also played a central role in the American Revolution, starting with the signing of the Declaration of Independence at Philadelphia in 1776. As the second state to ratify the Constitution, Pennsylvania joined the Union on December 12, 1787. The state's development was spurred by the agriculture of the Pennsylvania Germans, who had begun settling there in the late 1600s. In the 1800s coal and oil reserves were discovered and a steel industry was established.

212

**Question**: Why is Philadelphia's City Hall called the biggest penholder in the world?
**Answer**: Because the top of it holds a thirty-seven-foot tall statue of William Penn!

# Home of the Prairie Schooner

We're all so familiar with paved streets, roads, and superhighways that it's hard to imagine a time when there wasn't a single smooth, hard-surfaced travel route anywhere in America. Waterways were the first "highways" to pierce the wilderness. But they were sometimes too shallow for navigation or too rough, with swirling currents and dangerous rapids. And often the rivers, streams, and lakes didn't go where *people* wanted to go—across prairies and deserts, through forests, and over mountains.

The earliest land roads in America were Indian footpaths. After Europeans arrived, bringing horses, the footpaths became narrow pack-animal trails. Gradually the trails were widened to permit horse-drawn vehicles to pass through. But tree stumps, roots, and large rocks made these dirt roads extremely bumpy. Roads through low-lying areas became mud puddles in rainy weather and treacherous ice sheets during the deep freezes of winter. Horses suffered broken legs, and stagecoach passengers were often bruised and bleeding after a fairly short trip through quite flat country.

A group of pioneer farmers from Germany and Switzerland who, in the late 1600s, began to immigrate to southeastern Pennsylvania tried to think of a way to transport their families and their household goods over both wilderness roads and rivers and streams. Most of them were people of various Protestant sects, or subgroups, who shared similar religious beliefs and wanted to live in their own communities. They included Mennonites, Dunkards, Moravians, and Schwenkfelders. Best known among them were a people called the Amish. By the late 1700s so many of the newcomers had settled in Pennsylvania that people began to call them the Pennsylvania Dutch.

This was because they called themselves *Deutsch,* the German word for "German," which sounded to many Americans like "Dutch."

Each of the Pennsylvania German religious groups was bound together by its beliefs and practices. In general, these groups opposed war and did not use tobacco or alcohol. They did not engage in worldly amusements such as card playing and dancing. And they dressed in simple, unadorned clothing that earned them the name of "the plain people."

The Pennsylvania Germans worked hard at farming and stock raising and at all sorts of home and farm crafts. Pretty soon they had developed a special breed of large, strong horse well suited to pulling heavy loads. They named it the Conestoga horse, after Conestoga Township in Lancaster County, Pennsylvania, where most of them lived.

The Conestoga horse was perfect for pulling a plow or a well-loaded farm wagon. Even better, by the mid-1700s the Pennsylvania Germans had also designed a special long-distance freight wagon to be pulled by two or more teams of Conestoga horses. It was built in a boatlike shape that curved upward at both ends and had an arched white-canvas covering to protect the people, goods, and livestock riding inside. The interior of the covered wagon was about

AMISH CHILDREN

sixteen feet long and five feet wide, with plenty of headroom. It could hold thousands of pounds. Some people described it as "the belly of a whale" because it could swallow up so much. Others called it "the sea captain of the roads." The Pennsylvania Germans named it the Conestoga wagon.

Even though the plain people dressed in quiet, practical colors, they proudly painted their covered wagons in brilliant hues, usually bright blue on the underbody and red on the upper part of the body. But what really made the Conestoga wagon so special, aside from its capacity, was the way it could adapt to the terrible road conditions of the day.

First, it was sturdily built of specially selected wood that wouldn't splinter and crack at the first shaking up. Next, its wheels had broad rims for better traction in mud and on snow and ice. The wheels were widely spaced, too, to prevent the wagon's tipping over. And to keep from skidding down an icy hill, the rear wheels could be fitted with a metal ice cutter that snagged the ice and slowed the wagon's speed.

The curving ends of the Conestoga wagon, front and back, guaranteed that the contents wouldn't spill out when it was traveling up or down a steep grade. Best of all, if a stream or even a deep river had to be crossed, the wagon bed could be taken off its wheels and floated across like a boat. That was why the Conestoga wagon was also dubbed "the prairie schooner."

Most of the Pennsylvania Germans remained in Pennsylvania, but not all. Once the Conestoga wagon was invented, some began to head into Ohio, Indiana, and Illinois. They also established the largest Amish community west of the Mississippi, in Iowa, at a town called Kalona.

Mainly, though, the Pennsylvania-designed covered wagon was used by other pioneers of the 1800s as a means of traveling as far west as the Pacific Coast. And it served them well on roads that never amounted to much more than rough trails, dry riverbeds, or rugged mountain passes. The cross-continental journeys of these small worlds on wheels proved how expert the Pennsylvania Germans had been in adapting to their own wilderness existence of a hundred years earlier.

The Pennsylvania Germans may have clung to their old ways and remained, for the most part, a settled people who seldom left their established communities. But their skill at finding practical solutions to the problems of long-distance travel in America before the advent of the railroad was enormous. Untold numbers of people owed their pioneering successes to these hardworking farmers back in the home of the prairie schooner.

# RHODE ISLAND

Rhode Island, the smallest state in the Union, is not an island. Its Narragansett Bay does, however, contain a number of small islands, and one larger one with the Indian name of Aquidneck Island. Some historians think that it was the Italian sea captain Giovanni da Verrazano who named Aquidneck Rhode Island, after the Isle of Rhodes in the Aegean Sea. In any case, the name became that of the entire state.

The first white settlement, called Providence, was established by Roger Williams, a colonist who left Puritan-controlled Massachusetts to found a new colony where religious freedom could truly flourish. Williams purchased land from the Algonquian Indians of the region and, like William Penn in Pennsylvania, tried to maintain fair and friendly relations with the original inhabitants.

*Little Rhody,* as Rhode Island is nicknamed, measures only forty-eight miles from north to south and thirty-seven miles from east to west. Although it was the first of the Thirteen Colonies to declare itself independent from England, it was the last to ratify the United States Constitution, because of concerns for the rights of smaller state became the first to establish mills for the spinning and weaving of cotton, a prosperous industry that was to spread to other parts of New England. Today Rhode Island is a leading manufacturer of small metal products such as jewelry and silverware.

---

**Question**: If Rhode Island is the smallest state and Alaska is the largest, how many Rhode Islands would fit into Alaska?
**Answer**: It would take 475 Little Rhodys to make up an area the size of the state of Alaska.

---

217

# The Smuggled Secret of Samuel Slater

It's hard to imagine the daily life of a woman in colonial America without picturing her at her spinning wheel. There she spent long, monotonous hours drawing cotton lint or wool fleece or flax fibers into single strands of thread to weave into cloth on her loom.

What a pity that so much time in a life crowded with other household chores had to be spent on the tedious operation of spinning thread. In England, in the 1700s, inventors were already working on machines to do this job. And by 1769 Sir Richard Awkright patented one that could spin many strands of thread at one time. Awkright's invention also twisted the cotton strands to make them both stronger and finer than homespun cotton.

The Americans longed to have such a machine, especially in New England, where there were numerous rushing streams that could be harnessed to provide power that would run factories and mills of all sorts. But there was a catch. England forbade the export of manufacturing machinery. It wanted the colonies to send their cotton and other raw materials to the mother country. There the English would process the cotton into thread, weave it into cloth, and ship it back to America, making a handy profit on the finished product.

The colonists thought of various schemes for getting the plans to Arkwright's spinning machine and building it in America. Drawings of British inventions, however, weren't allowed out of the country, and even the workers in the textile industry were forbidden to leave. So one man from Philadelphia secretly arranged with a group of skilled English workmen to make him a set of brass models of Arkwright's machine and ship it to America. But that idea didn't succeed either. Customs officials at the London docks became suspicious, broke open the crate, and seized the contents.

Between 1775 and 1783 the colonies were at war with England. Although the American Revolution won the colonies their independence, the British were no closer to sharing their inventions for factory-made goods with the Americans. Anxious to start their own industries, some of the young states actually ran lotteries to provide prize money for the American invention of a successful cotton-spinning machine.

Then in 1789 the Americans had a stroke of good luck. A twenty-one-year-old Englishman by the name of Samuel Slater immigrated to the United States. Slater had been apprenticed at the age of fourteen to one of Sir Richard Awkright's partners in the textile industry, and he had learned all about the new cotton-spinning machinery. When he heard that the Americans were looking for such machinery, he began to memorize down to the last detail the plans for Awkright's machine. Then without telling anyone, he disguised himself as a farm boy and sailed for America.

Arriving in New York, the plans still safely stowed away in his head, Slater made his way to Rhode Island. There he met a Providence merchant named Moses Brown who was keenly interested in starting a cotton-spinning factory. Brown and his son-in-law, William Almy, put up the money and agreed that Slater should have a half-ownership in the business.

By 1790 Slater's amazing mind had delivered all the know-how for building a water-powered spinning machine, with dozens of spindles, in Pawtucket, Rhode Island, just north of Providence. Soon other cotton-spinning mills were built in the state. By the time of the War of 1812, there were 169 small factories spinning thread and weaving cloth in and around the Providence area. The secret that Samuel Slater had smuggled to America from England was out!

The development of cotton-spinning factories in the United States had two very far-reaching and not altogether happy effects. As soon as there were cotton mills on American soil, Southern planters looked for ways to increase cotton production. One of their main problems was the difficulty of separating the cotton seeds from the cotton fibers. Doing this job by hand, a slave could produce only about a pound of cleaned cotton a day.

Then in 1793 Eli Whitney invented the cotton gin. This machine made it possible for one person to turn out fifty pounds of cotton lint a day, using a small hand-turned gin. Large, water-powered ones turned out a thousand pounds a day. Planters quickly increased their cotton-growing acreage. This, in turn, led to an enormous increase in the number of African slaves brought to work the cotton fields. In fact, it firmly established the institution of slavery in the United States.

In the North, too, the labor picture was changed by the coming of the cotton mills. True, New England women might no longer have to put in long hours at home at their spinning wheels. Instead, however, it wasn't long before they found themselves working from dawn to dark in the New England textile factories.

At first those who worked in the factories were mainly the young daughters of farming families, wanting to earn a little money for a few years before leaving their jobs to get married. Most of the young women were between the ages of seventeen and twenty-four. The mill owners built dormitories for them to live in, where they were well supervised. "Mind-improving" lectures were given in the evenings, and church services were held on Sundays.

By the 1830s, though, conditions had changed for the worse. Unable to coax a living from the poor New England soil, farmers and

CHILD LABOR, 1909

new immigrants were flocking to the textile mills, which had expanded into Massachusetts and other nearby states. Entire families worked as long as thirteen hours a day, six days a week, living in crowded hovels beside the factories.

Worst of all, children as young as six were put to work tending the spinning machines. Their lives were broken by ill health and tragic accidents. Yet child labor would continue for many, many years in the textile and other industries, until it was effectively outlawed in the 1930s.

Like most forms of industrial progress, the coming of cotton-spinning machinery to America brought benefits to some and harsh injustices to others. Few of us can accurately foretell the future, and in 1789 most people looked on industrialization as an overall good. At the time that Samuel Slater smuggled his secret across the sea to Rhode Island, they thought little of the cruelties to which it might lead.

# SOUTH CAROLINA

CAPITAL: COLUMBIA

PALMETTO

Like North Carolina, South Carolina was once part of the larger territory known as Carolana, named for King Charles I of England. South Carolina's nickname is *The Palmetto State,* because of a victory over the British during the American Revolution. Defending themselves in a small island fortress made from native palmetto logs, a group of South Carolina patriots managed to destroy an invading British warship. This event took place in 1776, near Charleston Harbor. According to witnesses, the smoke that rose from the burning ship was in the shape of a feathery, fan-leaved palmetto tree.

Crop-growing Indians—mainly Catawba, Yamasee, and Cherokee—inhabited the area when Spanish and French explorers first appeared in the 1500s. Charleston, originally called Charles Town after King Charles II, was settled in the late 1600s. It soon became a major port for the shipment of rice and indigo (a plant that yields a blue dye) grown on the nearby lowland plantations by African slaves. Statehood for South Carolina came on May 23, 1788.

South Carolina was the first state to secede from the Union, in December 1860, on the eve of the Civil War. And the first shots of the war were fired upon the federal garrison of Fort Sumter, in Charleston Harbor, by Confederate troops on April 12, 1861. The war crippled South Carolina's plantation economy, which was by then based on the growing of cotton. After a long period of recovery, textile and other profitable industries were developed in the state.

223

**Question**: Is there really such a place as Catfish Row in Charleston, South Carolina?

**Answer**: Catfish Row is the name of a row of houses in the 1925 novel *Porgy* (later made into the folk opera *Porgy and Bess*). The author, DuBose Heyward, modeled Catfish Row on a group of *real* Charleston houses, Cabbage Row, where the black residents sold vegetables out of boxes on their windowsills.

# The Revolt of Denmark Vesey

Denmark Vesey could hardly believe his good luck. Again and again he carefully read the numbers on the lottery ticket he held in his hand. It was true! They were the same as the winning numbers posted in the East Bay Street lottery office in Charleston, South Carolina. All Denmark Vesey had to do was to go up to the window, present his ticket, and collect his money—the unimaginably large sum of fifteen hundred dollars.

This was a great deal of money for just about any ordinary person in South Carolina in the year 1799. But it was especially unusual for a black slave to come into such wealth. For one thing, very few slaves *had* any money of their own, much less enough to buy a lottery ticket. Also, most of the hundred thousand slaves who lived in South Carolina in the late 1700s labored on the rice, indigo, and cotton plantations, located some distance inland from the bustling port city of Charleston, where lottery tickets could be bought.

Denmark Vesey, however, was not a plantation slave. For eighteen years he'd belonged to a sea captain named Joseph Vesey. Captain Vesey was a slave trader who'd grown wealthy importing slaves from Africa to the Caribbean and the American South. In 1781, on one of his trips from the Danish colony of Saint Thomas to another Caribbean island, he'd picked up a fourteen-year-old youth whom he named Denmark. The boy became a personal servant to Captain Vesey and, as was the custom, he was given his master's second name.

. . . A FOURTEEN-YEAR-OLD

Between 1781 and 1783, Denmark Vesey sailed with the captain. He'd watched the bewildered and shackled blacks of West Africa driven aboard the slave ship and packed into tightly cramped quarters like so much cargo. He'd witnessed the filth, disease, and inhuman treatment that caused as many as one-third of the captives to die and be tossed overboard before the voyage was completed. And he'd seen the despair and humiliation of those who survived to reach port as they stood on the auction block, waiting to be sold to the highest bidder.

Then, as the American Revolution ended in 1783, things changed for the better for Denmark Vesey. The captain decided to retire from the slave trade. He moved to Charleston and went into the business of furnishing supplies for ships being readied to sail to ports all over the world. Denmark Vesey, as one of eight slave servants in the Captain's household, became a skilled carpenter. The captain even hired him out to other Charleston residents and gave him a little money in addition to his keep. This money enabled Denmark Vesey to try his luck in the lottery, and now the money he had won would take him a step further. With six hundred dollars he could buy his freedom from Captain Vesey and join the thousand or so free blacks who lived in the city of Charleston.

In January of 1800, a month after the lottery, the captain gave Denmark Vesey his papers of emancipation. With the remainder of his winnings he was able to buy himself a small house in Charleston. And along with other free blacks, who worked as cooks, nurses, seamstresses, bricklayers, fishermen, and blacksmiths, he was able to earn a living hiring himself out freely as a carpenter.

Life was much improved for Denmark Vesey. It was not perfect, of course, for free blacks did not share equal status with whites. They had to be very careful to carry their papers with them at all times lest they be resold into slavery. They had to pay special taxes for the privilege of living in Charleston, and if accused of a crime, they could not testify against a white person. So they banded together to protect themselves in special fellowship and church groups.

They also read and discussed the writings of the antislavery leaders of the day. Not all abolitionists lived in the northern states. In Charleston itself there were whites who opposed slavery. Among the

most outspoken were the Grimké sisters, Sarah and Angelina. And on the French-owned Caribbean island of St. Domingue, there had actually been a successful slave revolt in 1804. The now independent island republic was known as Haiti.

As Denmark Vesey thought of this event, he could not wipe from his memory the scenes he'd beheld on the slave ship of his former master. Infuriating too was the fact that in 1807 the importation of slaves into the United States had been declared illegal. Yet the law was not enforced, because the plantation owners who were profiting from the boom in cotton demanded more and more black slave labor.

By 1821 Denmark Vesey felt himself driven to take action. Carefully he began to enlist the help of cool, courageous, and well-organized blacks, some slave and some free. The network began to recruit support from within Charleston, at that time the sixth-largest city in the United States, and well beyond it. For Denmark Vesey planned nothing short of a rebellion that would free slaves not only in South Carolina but throughout the United States. He saw himself as favored by fortune in having become free, educated, and prosperous. Now, at the age of fifty-four, he must try to lift the burden that other Africans endured under slavery.

Vesey and other free blacks contributed money to buy weapons and horses, which were hidden away in readiness for the uprising. By the time a date—July 14, 1822—had been set for the revolt, there were said to be nine thousand followers secretly sworn to the movement.

But the revolt in Denmark Vesey's heart and mind was never to become a reality. Sometime in May 1822 word leaked out through a house slave who had been frightened and told his master. Vesey decided to move the date up from July 14 to June 16, in case there were any more leaks. But it was already too late. The Charleston authorities had been put on the alert.

Although the authorities were never able to identify most of the members of the movement, its leaders were caught and tried. On July 2, 1822, Denmark Vesey paid with his life for the freedom he had hoped to share with others. True, his plans had called for fighting violence with violence. But as the Civil War was to prove some forty years later, there was to be no peaceful way of ending human enslavement.

# SOUTH DAKOTA

CAPITAL: PIERRE

Like North Dakota, South Dakota was named for the Dakota, or Sioux, Indians, whose name meant "friends," or "allies." Early French claims to the region ended when the United States purchased the Louisiana Territory in 1803. The Lewis and Clark Expedition passed through South Dakota in 1804 on its way west, and again in 1806 on the return trip.

During the 1800s fur trading along the Missouri River and gold mining in the Black Hills brought settlements and finally statehood, on November 2, 1889. But agricultural development was slow, due to both "white blizzards"—snowstorms—and "black blizzards"—severe dust storms. The dust storms were brought on by long periods of drought that caused them to continue for years. South Dakota's nickname, *The Coyote State,* is a reminder of the large number of these small animals of the wolf family that once populated the plains.

Crops grown today in South Dakota include corn, oats, and rye. Stock raising is widespread, and gold is still being mined in the Black Hills, where it was first discovered in 1875. The Black Hills are also the site of the famed Mount Rushmore National Memorial. This major tourist attraction depicts, in carved granite sixty feet high, the faces of four United States presidents. It was created by Gutzon Borglum, an American of Danish descent, who worked on it from 1927 until his death in 1941.

**Question**: The heads of George Washington, Thomas Jefferson, Theodore Roosevelt, and Abraham Lincoln on the Mount Rushmore National Memorial are each as high as a five-story building. If the figures were carved from head to toe, how tall would each man be?

**Answer**: Each president would stand 465 feet tall, about the height of a forty-story building!

# Sitting Bull's Last Stand

In July 1876, as the United States was celebrating the one hundredth anniversary of its Declaration of Independence, word came of the death of General George Custer in the battle of the Little Bighorn, also known as Custer's Last Stand. The encounter between General Custer's cavalry and a large band of Sioux and Cheyenne Indians had taken place in far-off Montana, which was still a territory rather than a state. All of Custer's men, numbering more than two hundred, had died with their leader in the worst defeat the United States Army ever suffered at the hands of the Indians.

To this day little is known about what really happened at Montana's Little Bighorn River, where the battle was fought. And the man who brought down Custer himself was never identified. It *was* known, though, that the Indians had been fighting to hold on to their lands in the South Dakota and Montana regions, and to keep from being forced to live on reservations. So the blame for Custer's death was directed at two Indian chiefs, Crazy Horse of the Oglala Sioux and Sitting Bull of the Hunkpapa Sioux.

In 1877 Crazy Horse surrendered to American troops but was murdered shortly afterward. Sitting Bull, also hounded by government forces, fled to Canada, where he and his people remained for four years. "The Great Spirit

CHIEF
CRAZY HORSE

made me an Indian," Sitting Bull declared, "but not a reservation Indian—and I don't intend to become one!"

Since Sitting Bull's youth, life had changed drastically for the plains Indians. He'd been born near the Grand River in South Dakota territory in 1831, a time when buffalo hunting was still a way of life for the Sioux. From these wild herds the Indians obtained almost everything they needed—skins for clothing, blankets, and tepees; meat for food; fats for ointments; and horn and bone for tools and utensils. Dried buffalo dung served as fuel for their heating and cooking fires.

At the age of fourteen the young Sioux proved himself a brave warrior, and by the 1860s he was chief of the Hunkpapa Sioux, one of seven major groups that shared the plains. By the 1870s, however, changes that seriously threatened the Indians' survival had started to take place.

The building of the railroads and the discovery of gold in the South Dakota Black Hills brought white prospectors into buffalo-hunting territory. Travelers actually shot buffalo from the windows of the passing railroad cars for sport. Their meat was left to rot, and their hides, which sold for three dollars apiece in 1870, could be had for as little as sixty-five cents by 1875. In the next twenty-five years, nearly 15 million buffalo would be senselessly slaughtered by whites as part of the "taming" of the West.

Sitting Bull and his people remained in Canada until they could hold out no longer, for there too the buffalo and other game had all but disappeared and the government refused to help. Returning to the United States on July 19, 1881, the proud Indian chief surrendered and was held for two years as a prisoner of war at Fort Randall in South Dakota. His few hundred followers were sent to live on a South Dakota reservation where they were expected to survive as farmers, despite the poor growing soil and their lack of farming experience.

For Sitting Bull himself, another kind of life was waiting. Not long after he joined his people on the reservation in South Dakota, he was approached by Buffalo Bill Cody to become a feature attraction in Cody's Wild West Show. Buffalo Bill, whose real name was William Frederick Cody, had earned his nickname as a buffalo hunter, supplying meat for railroad-building crews in Kansas. He had also been a scout for government troops fighting Indians in the West. Then in the 1880s he'd gone into show business full-time, traveling the country doing reenactments of battles with Indians and putting on displays of stunt riding and shooting skills.

BUFFALO BILL CODY

Buffalo Bill stood for everything that Sitting Bull disliked about the white man's ruthless takeover of Indian lands. But life on the reservation was also hateful to him. So in 1885 he signed up with the Wild West Circus for a tour of the eastern United States. He received $125 plus a salary of $50 a week, and sold autographed copies of his photograph for 25 cents each. Crowds lined up to see him, for he had become a celebrity and was exhibited as "The Slayer of Custer." Although untrue, this billing must have pleased him, for he seemed to care little about the money he earned. In fact, he gave most of it away to the street urchins who waited outside the arena gates.

When the tour ended in 1886, Buffalo Bill urged Sitting Bull to continue on to England with the troupe. But Sitting Bull declined. He had grown tired of being an "exhibit" and felt too that such a role was damaging to the dignity of the Indian. Besides, he remarked, "White men talk too much ... like the noise of waters which man can't stop."

On parting, Buffalo Bill gave the Indian chief a present of a performing horse. On the cue of a gunshot, the horse would rise up on its hind legs and paw the air. The trick horse was to remain with Sitting Bull until his death in 1890.

Back on the reservations, conditions were worsening. The Indian lands were steadily reduced, epidemics of influenza and measles took many lives, and the meager government food rations consisted of bacon fat and biscuit, sugar and coffee. An Indian mystic named Wovoka began a religious movement that would supposedly bring back the buffalo and rid the plains of the white intruders. Through chants and shuffling dances, known as "ghost dancing," visions would appear that would become real. Wovoka's beliefs were not a direct military threat, nor was Sitting Bull involved in the movement. But the Indian chief's power among the Sioux was still feared. Suppose he did start an uprising?

Early on the morning of December 15, 1890, forty-three Indian policemen backed by government troops came to arrest Sitting Bull. He protested valiantly, refusing to leave his people. In the confusion a shot rang out, possibly fired by one of Sitting Bull's followers. Instantly one of the Indian policemen shot and killed Sitting Bull. At that moment Sitting Bull's horse, tethered beside his hut, reared up and fiercely pawed the air. The Indians on both sides shrank back in alarm. They were convinced that the proud spirit of Sitting Bull had entered the body of the animal.

The death of Sitting Bull sounded a final note of defeat in the Indians' struggle for a return to their former way of life. Even Buffalo Bill was saddened when the horse, now without a master, was returned to him to continue performing in the Wild West Show.

Sitting Bull was buried at a government fort in North Dakota. But in 1953 the Sioux demanded that his body be returned to the place in South Dakota where he had been killed in 1890. It rests today near the town of Mobridge, where Sitting Bull made his courageous last stand on behalf of his people.

A SIOUX WARRIOR'S GRAVE

# TENNESSEE

"Tennessee" probably comes from the name of a large Cherokee village known as Tanasi. Nobody is quite sure what the word itself means. Spanish, French, and English explorers reached the area starting in the 1500s. But the first permanent white settler was a man named William Bean, who built a cabin on the Watauga River in the northeastern part of the region in 1768. During the American Revolution the Watauga settlement was a county of neighboring North Carolina. Tennessee became a state of the Union on June 1, 1796.

Tennessee's nickname *The Volunteer State* refers to its generous contribution of fighting men in the War of 1812 and again in the Mexican War of 1846–48. Another nickname, *The Big Bend State,* describes the strange, lopsided U-shaped course of the Tennessee River.

Tennessee stretches for over 430 miles from east to west, but it measures only 110 miles from north to south. The middle and western portions of the state are more level and fertile than the eastern part. Middle Tennessee is the home of the famous Tennessee walking horse, prized for pleasure riding. Nashville, the center of the country-and-western music industry, is also located there. Memphis, on the Mississippi River in western Tennessee, is "the home of the blues." It is also the city where Elvis Presley grew up and is the site of his home, Graceland, and his grave.

234

---

**Question**: Part of Tennessee was once known as the State of Franklin, named for Benjamin Franklin. When and why?

**Answer**: Between 1784 and 1788 the Watauga settlement was no longer part of North Carolina. It formed its own "state" with its own governor and called itself Franklin, but it was never admitted to the Union. Franklin was a state without a country!

---

# Casey Jones and the *Cannonball Express*

*Come all you rounders, I want you to hear,*
*The story told of a brave engineer. . . .*

So begins "The Ballad of Casey Jones," one of the most famous of all railroading songs. But unlike "I've Been Working on the Railroad" or "Chattanooga Choo-choo," "Casey Jones" is a true story about a real person.

John Luther Jones was born in Jordan, Kentucky, in 1864. He took the name Casey from the Kentucky town of Cayce, where he grew up, before becoming a railroad man and settling in Jackson, Tennessee. Casey's run was on the *Cannonball Express*, a fast mail train of the Illinois Central. The entire rail line ran from Chicago to New Orleans. But Casey's route covered just the part of the journey from Memphis, Tennessee, to Canton, Mississippi—188 miles—and then back again. All along the track people knew it was Casey at the controls by the way he blew the whistle—soft, then shrieky, and then fading away. It was a creepy, middle-of-the-night sound. But the story goes that folks took comfort in it. "There goes Casey," they'd murmur, "and the *Cannonball Express*."

Casey was well over six feet tall, almost always wore a broad grin, and was happiest of all when he got his engine up to top speed. He was known as a "fast roller," sure to get his train in on time. "Yet," as one of his fellow trainmen wrote of him, "he had a reputation as a safe engineer." In a day when train wrecks were common, he'd had only a few minor derailments, so he "was either lucky, or else his judgment was as nearly perfect as human judgment can be."

On the rainy Sunday of April 29, 1900, Casey had just finished his northbound run from Mississippi into Memphis. He was about to go off duty when he learned that the engineer scheduled for the southbound run was sick. Could Casey take the southbound train back down to Mississippi, even though it was already an hour and a half behind time?

Casey was the last person in the world to say no to a challenge like that. He vowed he'd do it *and* make up the lost time, provided he could have his regular engine, Number 382. Soon Casey and his black fireman, Sim Webb, were roaring down the track. Sim shoveled in the coal and Casey built up speed. The whistle shrieked.

> *. . . And the switchmen knew by the engine's moans*
> *That the man at the throttle was Casey Jones. . . .*

The train was loaded with passengers, mail, and freight, and it was nighttime and rainy. But Casey continued to highball his way south

as Sim kept the engine hot. They'd actually covered the first fifty miles at better than a mile a minute, and it looked like they were going to make up every lost minute by the time they reached Canton, Mississippi.

The *Cannonball* was still barreling along as they got toward the town of Vaughan, fourteen miles short of Canton. It was close to four A.M., and they were running only a few minutes behind time. "Oh, Sim," Casey shouted delightedly, "the old girl's got her high-heeled slippers on tonight!" As Sim Webb later reported, those were the last words that Casey Jones ever spoke. Just as the *Cannonball* came around the curve approaching the Vaughan station, the cars of a freight train loomed on the main track. The freight had been unable to pull completely off onto the siding because of a stalled train in front of it. And no signal had been relayed to Casey before he saw the red lights of the freight train's caboose.

Sim had time only to yell to Casey, "Look out! We're gonna hit something." Then he quickly lowered himself from the engine cab and jumped, hoping that Casey had too.

But Casey Jones didn't jump. He remained in the cab, applying all his strength to the air-brake lever. Even so, Casey could not stop the train in time. In fact, the engine went right through the caboose, into a freight car filled with corn, and into another one filled with hay. It stopped just short of one filled with lumber.

The cab of Number 382 was demolished. But the engine stayed on the track, and so did all the passenger and freight cars behind it. Casey's slowing of the engine had prevented a major crash and derailment.

Sim Webb recovered from his jump from the moving train, and not a single crew or passenger life was lost, except, of course, for that of Casey Jones. Some say he was found in the wreckage, his hand still on the brake. Others tell that he was thrown clear, every bone in his body broken. And so "The Ballad of Casey Jones" ends with the lines

*Fireman jumped off, but Casey stayed on.*
*He's a good engineer, but he's dead and gone.*

The ballad itself was written by Wallace Saunders, a black engine wiper who'd known Casey and, like so many others, was deeply touched by the sacrifice he'd made in giving up his own life to save those of his passengers and crew.

Casey's wife and three children went on living for many years in the one-story house Casey had bought in Jackson, Tennessee, back in 1893. Today it's known as the Casey Jones Home and Railroad Museum, for a sister engine to Jones's favorite Number 382 is on display, along with other railroading mementos. They include the watch that Casey was wearing, its hands stopped forever by the impact of the fatal crash of the engine of the *Cannonball Express.*

# TEXAS

CAPITAL: AUSTIN

"Texas" comes from *tejas,* the Spanish version of a Caddo Indian word meaning "friends," or "allies." The Caddo people themselves are said to have used this word as a greeting or sign of welcome. The region was first visited by gold-seeking Spaniards in the 1500s. Although no gold was found, forts and missions were built and, along with Mexico, the Texas territory became a possession of Spain.

Mexico gained its independence from Spain in 1821, and Texas then became part of the Republic of Mexico. But already Anglo-Americans from the United States were forming settlements there. In 1836, following a defeat at the mission chapel known as the Alamo, Texans regrouped and in a surprise attack overcame the Mexican troops. For nine years, until 1845, Texas was an independent republic. It became a state of the Union on December 29, 1845. Its nickname, *The Lone Star State,* commemorates the single star in the flag it flew as an independent nation.

THE ALAMO

Until Alaska joined the Union in 1959, Texas was the largest state. Big is still the word for Texas. It's a big producer of oil and gas, of food crops and cotton, of livestock and space technology. Its wide-open spaces have been home to cowboys and cattle drives. And even today Texas boasts the largest privately owned ranch in the world, the King Ranch, which is roughly equal in size to the state of Rhode Island!

---

**Question**: Which of the contiguous states is bigger than all of Spain, bigger than all of France, and bigger than New York, Pennsylvania, Massachusetts, Ohio, Illinois, and Wisconsin all put together?

**Answer**: Texas. As the travelers of an earlier day used to say:
*"The sun has riz, the sun has set,*
*And here we is, in Texas yet!"*

---

# Cowboys on the Chisholm Trail

Probably few people in America had ever heard the word cowboy until right after the Civil War. And certainly nobody had ever heard of the Chisholm Trail until after a part-Cherokee Indian trader by the name of Jesse Chisholm started a wagon route from Texas to Kansas in 1865.

Very soon the Chisholm Trail became a cattle trail, and a mounting swell of animals and herders began to travel north on it. For in order to get the numerous Texas cattle to markets in the East, the herds had to be walked from southern Texas to the nearest railroad depots, which were six to seven hundred miles away, in Kansas cow towns such as Abilene, Wichita, and Dodge City.

How did Texas get to have so many cattle in the first place? Most were half-wild Spanish longhorns that had been introduced to Texas back in the days when it was part of Mexico. Others were the gentler

English breeds, such as shorthorns and Herefords, that American settlers from the East had brought to Texas. While many Texans were off fighting in the Civil War, the various breeds had multiplied and fattened on the rich Texas grasslands. Now, after the war, there was a growing population all over the United States that was hungry for beef.

By 1868 the long drives were well under way. Herds of twenty-five hundred to three thousand cattle were common. Some were much larger. The animals might be strung out for a mile or more along the trail, under the watchful eyes of only a dozen or so mounted cowhands. The drives were slow moving, partly because they were so large and clumsy and partly because the cattlemen wanted the animals to fatten on the summer grasses as they moved toward the railroad weighing yards.

So for two to three months the trail crews lived in the open, eating meals from a traveling chuck wagon and sleeping under the stars. But they seldom had a chance to relax, because of the many hazards of the trail. Stampedes, rustlers, and fast-spreading diseases such as the dread tick fever could take a heavy toll, as could a sudden storm or rampaging river. Almost anything could start a stampede among the nervous longhorns—a shot in the night, a marauding wild animal, a gang of cattle rustlers, even the smell of water, if the animals were thirsty.

We tend to think of the cowboys who did this hard, tedious, and dangerous job as looking like the movie stars of the typical Hollywood western. But at least ten thousand of the thirty-five thousand cowboys of the 1860s and 1870s were Mexicans or blacks. Just as it was the Spanish who first brought the horse to America, it was the Mexican vaquero (from *vaca,* or "cow") who first began tending cattle from horseback. The English word "buckaroo," meaning cowboy or broncobuster, comes directly from the Spanish *vaquero.*

Many other words that have to do with western cattle raising have Spanish roots. "Corral" is from the Spanish for an enclosure, or yard; "lariat" is from *la reata;* and "lasso" is from *lazo,* a loop or snare. *Hacienda* is Spanish for ranch; "stampede" is from *estampida;* and "vamoose" comes from *vamos,* or "let's go."

The Mexican cowboys were mainly of mixed Spanish and Indian

BOSE IKARD

blood and had been in the region for a long time. As for the black cowboys, most had either been brought west as slaves before the Civil War or had arrived after the war as freemen looking for a better life. Many were already skilled in handling horses, having done so for their former masters.

One of the best-known black cowboys was Bose Ikard. He'd been born a slave in Mississippi in 1847. When he was five years old, his master moved his entire household to Texas. Bose Ikard grew up to be a skilled cowpuncher and was hired out to other cattlemen and trail bosses. He made his name working with Colonel Charles Goodnight, the designer of the traveling chuck wagon and the founder (with Oliver Loving) of the Goodnight-Loving Trail, which ran slightly west of the Chisholm. When Ikard died in 1929, Goodnight placed a stone marker on his grave at Weatherford, Texas, praising the man who had ridden with him "in many stampedes," never failing to show "splendid behavior."

At the end of the trail, after each of the long drives, the cowboys received their pay envelopes of a hundred dollars or so. Who could resist a spree in one of the rowdy railhead cow towns, with their saloons, dance halls, and gambling houses? Most cowboys probably returned to Texas broke and ready to do ranch work until the next year's cattle drive began.

Maybe it was just as well that by the 1880s homesteaders had begun fencing in the open rangelands and that the railroads had started coming closer and closer to the Texas cattle spreads. The boom in Texas cattle raising continued. But after less than twenty years, the long drives were little more than a memory for the hard-riding, hard-working black, white, and Hispanic cowboys of the trail.

# UTAH

The Ute Indians, a hunting and food-gathering people, are believed to have given Utah its name. Spanish visitors who passed through the region in the 1500s and again in the 1700s were followed by American fur trappers in the early 1800s. The earliest permanent white settlers were the Mormons, a persecuted religious group led by Brigham Young, who were searching for a new home. The first small party of pioneers arrived in 1847, and large numbers soon followed. Statehood was delayed, however, until January 4, 1896, because of the Mormon practice of permitting a man to be married to more than one wife at the same time. The Mormon church ordered this practice stopped in 1890. Today seventy percent of Utah's inhabitants are of the Mormon faith.

Promontory Point in northern Utah was the site of the "meeting

MAY 10, 1869

244

of the rails," on May 10, 1869. There the Union Pacific and Central Pacific railroads were joined, providing the first coast-to-coast rail service in the country. Utah's many famed tourist attractions include Arches, Bryce Canyon, and Zion national parks, all with fantastic natural stone formations.

Utah's nickname, *The Beehive State,* reflects the hard work and industry of the Mormon settlers who irrigated the land for farming and built Salt Lake City. The city is famous for its imposing buildings and monuments. The Sea Gull Monument in Temple Square is a tall column topped with the gilded figures of two sea gulls. It commemorates the cricket infestation of 1848, during which flocks of sea gulls from the Great Salt Lake appeared, devouring the crickets and saving the crops.

**Question**: What is the second saltiest body of water in the world, after the Dead Sea?

**Answer**: Utah's Great Salt Lake. Except for a species of small brine shrimp, no fish can live in it, for it is four to seven times saltier than the ocean. It's also the largest lake in the United States west of the Mississippi River.

# All Those Dinosaur Bones

"At last in the top of the ledge . . . I saw eight of the tail bones of a *Brontosaurus* in exact position. It was a beautiful sight." Who else could have written words like this in a diary but a paleontologist, a scientist who studies prehistoric life?

The paleontologist was Earl Douglass from the Carnegie Museum in Pittsburgh, Pennsylvania, where he was already building an outstanding collection of dinosaur remains. It was August of 1909 when Douglass came upon the wonderful find in the northeastern corner of Utah, near the border with Colorado. What had brought him to this distant, rugged, mountain-and-canyon region in the torrid heat of summer?

Douglass knew that similar rock formations in the American West had yielded dinosaur skeletons. He felt that this area too would be rich in fossils of the "terrible lizards," which is how the word dinosaur translates from the Greek. And he was right, for here were bones and teeth from the bony-plated Stegosaurus, the gigantic Brontosaurus (also known as Apatosaurus), the sharp-toothed and sharp-clawed meat-eating Allosaurus, and a number of other dinosaur relatives.

All together, there were fossils from about ten kinds of dinosaurs that had lived in the Jurassic, or middle, Period of dinosaur life, about 140 million years ago. Even more exciting, as Douglass was to discover, this single magnificent sandstone cliff in Utah held one of the largest concentrations of fossilized dinosaur bones in the world!

How did so many dinosaur specimens come together all in one place? Douglass's studies and those of other paleontologists revealed that millions of years ago a river had run through the area. Many dinosaurs lived and died near its banks, which often overflowed. The waters washed the dinosaur remains down the river. Their flesh and other soft parts decayed, but their bony parts were eventually buried beneath layers of sand and gravel in the river bottom or along its banks.

More millions of years went by. The river vanished, but other waterways came and went. They deposited layers of sand and mud that absorbed minerals from the water, hardening the deposits into rock. The dinosaur bones buried far beneath the surface also absorbed minerals and hardened into fossils.

Then, to the east of this region, the Rocky Mountains slowly began to heave up out of the Earth's crust. As they did, the dinosaur burial grounds began to be squeezed and tilted upward. Gradually those grounds also rose to form rocky ledges and sharp peaks—not, of course, as high as the Rockies themselves. Once these peaks were exposed to rain, snow, frost, and wind, their surfaces began to wash

away or crack off, exposing the fossils within. That was how the eight perfectly aligned tailbones of the long-buried Brontosaurus that Douglass found in 1909 had come into view.

In 1915 President Woodrow Wilson heard about the dinosaur-rich quarry that Douglass had started digging in Utah, and he proclaimed the site part of the National Park Service. It was given the name of Dinosaur National Monument. The park itself sprawls for 325 square miles, about two thirds of it lying across the Utah border in Colorado. But there is only *one* place at Dinosaur National Monument where dinosaur fossils have been found and where you can actually see thousands of them.

That place is at the Dinosaur Quarry Visitor Center in the Utah section of the park, seven miles north of the town of Jensen. Although many dinosaur bones and even complete skeletons have been extracted from the area and placed in museums, more than twenty-three hundred bones have been left in the sandstone face of the quarry wall. This wall actually forms part of the Visitor Center, and there each summer Quarry paleontologists painstakingly scrape away at the stone to bring more and more fossils into high relief. Some stand away from the wall so that they are at least half rounded—leg bones and hip bones, foot bones and tailbones, armored plates and toothy skulls. They come from plant eaters and meat eaters. They represent dinosaurs ranging from "dainty" fifteen-foot-long, two-footed ornithopods to monstrous, seventy-foot-long, four-footed sauropods.

The mystery remains as to what really happened about 65 million years ago to wipe out the dinosaurs all over the world. Even the discoveries made at Dinosaur National Monument don't offer many clues. Did the weather become too hot, too cold, too wet, too dry? Did an asteroid crash into Earth, its dust blotting out the sun for months, or did a nearby star explode, showering down deadly radiation? Did the meat-eating dinosaurs kill off the plant-eating dinosaurs, and did the early mammals then eat the eggs of the meat-eating dinosaurs? We don't even know what colors dinosaurs were or how old they got to be before they died natural deaths.

But because of all those bones found in the wrinkled and upthrust cliffs and peaks of Utah and in other dinosaur graveyards, we do know a great deal about their size, their shape, what they ate, and even the kind of world they must have lived in.

# VERMONT

CAPITAL: MONTPELIER

*V*ert *mont,* the French words for "green mountain," gave Vermont its name. This was how the French explorer Samuel de Champlain described the region when he first visited it in 1609. Vermont's nickname, *The Green Mountain State,* also refers to the forested mountain range that runs the entire length of the state.

SAMUEL DE CHAMPLAIN

Indians of the Iroquois and Algonquian families hunted, gathered the sap of the maple tree, and farmed small patches of land in summer. White settlement began in the 1700s. But a conflict soon arose over the right of colonists from neighboring New York to own land in the Vermont region, which was officially claimed as part of New Hampshire. To defend their lands, the Vermonters organized the Green Mountain Boys, led by the fiery Ethan Allen, in 1771. Later, during the American Revolution, the Green Mountain Boys fought fiercely against the British.

Between 1777 and 1791, Vermont was actually an independent republic. For a short time it called itself New Connecticut. Then it changed its name to Vermont. It coined its own money, made its own laws, and was the first government in colonial America to officially ban slavery, on July 2, 1777. Vermont became a state of the Union on March 4, 1791. It was the first to be added to the thirteen states that had formerly been colonies.

Among the New England states, Vermont is the only one without a seacoast and is also smallest in population. The marble from its

250

quarries is famous, as is its maple sugar and maple syrup. And its picture-postcard rural scenery attracts tourists in all seasons of the year.

---

**Question**: Vermont is one of three states that were independent republics before becoming states. What are the other two?

**Answer**: Hawaii and Texas.

---

# Father Coolidge Swears In a President

New Englanders, especially those from Vermont, are said to be self-reliant, independent, and thrifty. If that is so, then Calvin Coolidge, the thirtieth president of the United States, was a perfect Vermonter.

He was born on the Fourth of July, 1872, in the tiny village of Plymouth Notch in central Vermont. His father, John Calvin Coolidge, was a farmer, a storekeeper, a justice of the peace, and the holder of other public offices in Vermont.

Cal, as he came to be called, learned much about politics from the elder Coolidge. After becoming a lawyer, he was elected to several high public offices, including the governorship of Massachusetts. And in 1920 Calvin Coolidge became vice president of the United States, in the administration of President Warren G. Harding.

Harding and Coolidge were about as different as two people could be. Harding was a hearty, easygoing ex-newspaper editor from Ohio. He loved fellowship, good times, and a big cigar. It was rumored that even though there was a law prohibiting the manufacture and sale of alcohol in the United States, the Harding White House secretly served liquor to guests.

Coolidge, on the other hand, was slight in stature, had a rather pinched face, and seldom smiled. Some went so far as to say that he looked like he'd been sucking on a pickle. Unlike Harding, Coolidge was not fond of large parties and believed in speaking as few words as possible. Soon after he became vice president, he was nick-named "Silent Cal."

People actually made bets to see how much conversation they could have with him. Once, at a White House dinner party, a woman seated beside him told him she'd bet that she could get more than two words out of him. Coolidge gave her a cool glance and replied, "You lose."

Life as vice president wasn't too demanding in the early 1920s, and Coolidge went back home to Vermont fairly often. He especially liked to escape the summer heat in Washington, D.C. So August of 1923 found Cal on vacation at his father's farmhouse in Plymouth Notch. The old family house had no electricity or telephone. The elder Coolidge could have afforded a telephone, but he saw no need for it. And Cal, who was just as frugal as his father, thought that was just fine. He didn't want busybody telephoners *or* visitors, for that matter.

Meantime, President Harding wasn't in Washington either. He was off on a long speaking trip to Alaska. He was still away when a secret message, written in code, reached him. It told of a serious scandal that was about to break in Washington. As a result of all the political favors that the jovial Harding had handed out, oil leases on public lands had been granted to private individuals in return for large sums of money. The United States Senate had found out about the corrupt goings-on under Harding and was about to start an investigation.

Coolidge, of course, knew nothing of these dealings. He did attend cabinet meetings, but he didn't spend time in the smoke-filled back rooms with Harding and his cronies. Harding was deeply upset by what he saw as betrayal by his friends. On the train back from Alaska he stopped in Seattle, where he was rumored to have had an attack of food poisoning. By the time he reached San Francisco, he was said to have contracted pneumonia. Then suddenly, on August 2, 1923, the fifty-seven-year-old Harding was dead. Some said it was suicide, some even whispered he had been poisoned. The true cause of his death was never learned, but most probably it was a combination of a bad heart, careless living, and the horror of losing his popularity once the scandal broke.

From the moment the news of Harding's illness in Seattle had

come east over the telegraph wires, a group of five newspaper and magazine reporters camped out at a small country inn at Ludlow, Vermont, some miles south of Plymouth Notch. They sniffed the possibility that Harding might not recover, and they wanted to be within reach of the vice president when the news came. They knew that Coolidge would never have permitted them to camp on his doorstep.

Sure enough, shortly past midnight, on August 3, 1923, one of the reporters received a phone call from his newspaper, the Boston *Post.* Word had just come through from San Francisco that President Harding had died. Calvin Coolidge was going to be the next president of the United States. Somebody had to get the news to him.

In the middle of the night, the five reporters roused the driver of an aged and wheezing rental car. The reporters jumped in and began a jolting, hilly ride on pitch-black country roads to the Coolidge farmhouse. A light appeared in the gloom. It was the kerosene lamp Father Coolidge kept lit in the farmhouse parlor for when he rose before daybreak to milk the cows. There was no doorbell and the front door was unlocked, as usual. The Boston *Post* reporter pushed open the door to the barking of the Coolidge collie dog. "Who is there?" Father Coolidge called out.

"The newspaper men," the reporter replied. "President Harding is dead. We must see your son at once."

Around three o'clock that morning, by the light of the kerosene lamp, Father Coolidge, as a justice of the peace and notary public, administered the oath of office of president of the United States to Calvin Coolidge. Then, according to his own report, the new President went back to bed—and fell asleep!

No president had ever been sworn into office by his own father or by such a minor official. There was some question as to whether Father Coolidge *could* swear in public servants other than those of the state of Vermont. So a few weeks later, just to be on the safe side, another swearing-in ceremony took place in Washington, D.C. It was presided over by a Supreme Court justice.

Coolidge didn't change at all after he became president. He finished out the Harding term and was elected to his own four-year term in 1924 with the slogan "Keep cool with Coolidge." Although he cleared the corrupt Harding people out of government, he pretty much let the country run itself, declaring, "The business of America is business."

The President's wife, Grace, had a warm, friendly personality that took care of social matters at the White House. Cal, meantime, made unannounced visits to the kitchen to make sure no food was being wasted or pilfered. Although the rest of the nation was on a good-times binge during the "Jazz Age" of the 1920s, the President continued his frugal ways. Once, when he was told that the White House roof needed fixing at a cost of half a million dollars, he rejected the repair with the remark, "If it's as bad as you say it is, why doesn't it fall down?"

Although Coolidge hated to authorize the spending of money, he didn't seem to care what others did. Americans were recklessly putting money into the stock market, which would collapse in 1929, leaving them with worthless stocks and huge debts. The great economic depression of the 1930s would follow.

It's doubtful, though, that Silent Cal foresaw any of this in 1928, when he was asked if he would run for reelection. He would almost certainly have won, for people liked his hands-off policy and admired his solid Vermont virtues. True to his habit of speaking as little as possible, Coolidge simply handed reporters slips of paper which read "I do not choose to run for President in 1928."

As Coolidge and his family were about to leave the White House early in 1929 to make way for the incoming president, Herbert Hoover, reporters finally coaxed a few words out of him. "Good-bye," Coolidge answered in his usual reserved and understated manner. "I have had a very enjoyable time in Washington."

Calvin Coolidge died on January 5, 1933, as the nation was experiencing the worst years of the Depression. He is buried at his birthplace and boyhood home of Plymouth Notch, Vermont. The old farmhouse can still be visited and looks much as it did on the night his father swore him in by lamplight as the thirtieth president of the United States.

# VIRGINIA

IROQUOIS

Virginia once covered a much larger territory than the state does now. It was named for Queen Elizabeth I of England, who never married and was known as the Virgin Queen. The state's nickname, *The Old Dominion*, comes from the mid-1600s, when as a colonial possession it remained loyal to the English king, Charles II, during a time of unrest for the English crown. Indians of the Algonquian, Siouan, and Iroquois families inhabited the Virginia region when the English made their first permanent settlement in the New World, at Jamestown in 1607. The "starving time" in the winter of 1609–10 nearly drove the men back to England. But tobacco growing, which they'd learned from the Indians, the arrival of wives, and the importation of black slaves in 1619 kept the settlement going.

Virginia was the home of such figures of the American Revolution as Patrick Henry (". . . give me liberty or give me death!"), Thomas Jefferson, who wrote the Declaration of Independence, and George Washington, who led the Continental Army to victory over the British. Virginia became a state of the Union on June 25, 1788. Like three other states—Kentucky, Massachusetts, and Pennsylvania—it officially calls itself a commonwealth, meaning a group of people banded together for the common good.

During the Civil War, Richmond was the capital of the Confederacy and Virginia was the war's central battleground. After a long period of recovery, manufacturing rather than agriculture became the state's main source of wealth. Virginia's famed tourist sites include the homes of Washington and Jefferson, the restored colonial capital of Williamsburg, and the scenic beauty of the Blue Ridge Mountains in the western part of the state.

---

**Question**: Why is Virginia "the mother of presidents"?

**Answer**: Four of the first five United States presidents—Washington, Jefferson, James Madison, and James Monroe—were Virginians. In addition, four more were born there, making a total of eight. They were William Henry Harrison, John Tyler, Zachary Taylor, and Woodrow Wilson.

---

# Robert E. Lee Makes a Painful Decision

On an April day in 1861, Robert E. Lee sat down at his writing desk in his home in Arlington, Virginia. He was about to put into words, in a letter to his sister, the most painful decision he had ever been called on to make.

"My Dear Sister," Lee began, ". . . we are in a state of war which will yield to nothing." Lee, who held the rank of colonel in the United States Army, was writing about the Civil War. The date on his letter was April 20, and just eight days earlier, on April 12, the opening guns of the war had been fired. The Confederate forces of the South had attacked the federal garrison of Fort Sumter in the harbor of Charleston, South Carolina.

ROBERT E. LEE

"The whole South is in a state of revolution," Lee went on, "into which Virginia . . . has been drawn; and though I recognize no necessity for this state of things . . . I had to meet the question whether I should take part against my native State."

Robert E. Lee wasn't the only American whose loyalties were divided as the nation split into opposing halves. Many people felt themselves of two minds. The war had started mainly over the question of whether a state had the right to secede from the Union. But an important issue, close to the surface, was that of slavery.

Although he was a Southerner, Virginia-born Robert E. Lee did not believe in slavery and, long before the war, he had freed the slaves he had inherited. Further, Lee did not believe that a state should secede from the Union. He had graduated from the United States Military Academy at West Point and had been the superintendent of the Academy for three years, and he had fought loyally for the country in the Mexican War.

But now, as he wrote in his letter, he found himself unable "to raise my hand against my relatives, my children, my home." Lee's handsome Arlington mansion was the family home of his wife, Mary Custis, a great-granddaughter of Martha Washington, and his seven children had grown up there. Remaining in the Union Army would have meant that Lee would instantly become the enemy of all those in Virginia that he loved.

"I have therefore," he wrote, "resigned my commission in the Army, and save in defense of my native State . . . I hope I may never be called on to draw my sword."

Lee's hope was not to be borne out. The South needed military commanders, and soon he was given the rank of general, leading Confederate troops into battle against officers and men who had once been his comrades in arms. Just as Lee, the Southerner, did not support slavery, there were those Northerners who did. The famous Union general William Tecumseh Sherman, who ravished Georgia, had actually stated in 1860 that "The negro must be the subject of the white man. Two such races cannot live in harmony save as master and slave." This was one of the great mockeries that made the Civil War, with its toll of over six hundred thousand lives, such a tragedy for the nation.

For over two years the war shifted back and forth, with Lee making many gains and even leading Confederate troops into the Union states of Maryland and Pennsylvania. But then came the turning point. Soon Union forces were threatening Richmond, the capital of Virginia *and* of the Confederate States of America.

Richmond had been chosen as the Confederate capital because it had flour mills, as well as ironworks for the production of guns and ammunition. So it was the main target of the Union Army. But the city was overburdened almost from the start of the war. It was where the Confederate wounded from the Virginia battlefields were cared for. Churches, schools, and private homes were converted into hospitals. Soon wood and coal for heating in winter became scarce, and the price of food and clothing skyrocketed. Flour rose to sixteen dollars a barrel, butter to three dollars a pound, and salt went from five cents to seventy cents a pound. Once the Union Army laid siege to Richmond, shortages of fuel, food, and clothing became even more severe.

Finally, on April 2, 1865, Lee announced that the city could hold out no longer. At once its citizens took what belongings they could and prepared to flee from the oncoming Yankees. Others set fire to the tobacco warehouses and blew up the remaining munitions stores. The entrance of Union troops the following day actually helped put an end to the destruction.

A week later, on April 9, General Robert E. Lee formally surrendered to General Ulysses S. Grant, the Union commander in chief, in the parlor of a privately owned house at a village called Appomattox Court House, west of Richmond. Lee asked that his men be allowed to keep their horses, as they needed them for spring plowing. Grant agreed. Grant also sent food supplies to Lee's tattered and starving army. And when his men began firing a cannon to celebrate their victory, Grant stopped them with the reminder that "the rebels are our countrymen again."

GENERAL GRANT

But the wounds of war were not to be quickly healed. Lee himself lost the Arlington house in which he had lived until 1861 and where he had written his letter to his sister. Because of its location on the Potomac River directly across from Washington, D.C., the house was occupied by Union troops during the Civil War. And in 1864, the estate was seized by the federal government on the grounds that the taxes had not been paid *in person* by the owner during the war.

By the time Lee's eldest son successfully sued for the return of the property, thousands of graves covered its grounds—it had been established, in 1864, as Arlington National Cemetery. Today the Custis-Lee Mansion with its tall white columns still sits on the cemetery and is known as the Robert E. Lee Memorial.

Lee, who died in 1870 at the age of sixty-seven, did not regret the painful decision he had made at the start of the Civil War. What he did regret all his life was the necessity for war. "It is well," he once remarked on the morning of yet another bloody battle, "that war is so terrible—we would grow too fond of it."

THE SACK OF RICHMOND

# WASHINGTON

CAPITAL: OLYMPIA

Washington is named for George Washington. It is the only state that honors a United States president in this way. One of its nicknames, *The Chinook State,* refers to the Chinook Indians, who lived near the mouth of the Columbia River. Another nickname, *The Evergreen State,* describes the magnificent forests of the Cascade Mountains. This north-south range divides Washington into a moist, western sector and a drier, eastern region. Mount Rainier, a 14,410-foot dormant volcanic peak covered with a cap of glacial ice, is the tallest in the Cascades and in the state.

Washington was once part of the larger territory known as the Oregon country. Spanish and English seafarers were the first Europeans to visit its coast. American claims began with Captain Robert Gray's discovery of the Columbia River, in 1792, and the Lewis and Clark overland expedition to the region, in 1805.

Many gold seekers, attracted to Idaho during the 1860 gold strike, continued on to Washington to become fur trappers and loggers. The population grew so slowly, however, that Washington didn't become a state until November 11, 1889. That same year the young city of Seattle, built mainly of wood, was destroyed by the Great Fire.

However, it was soon rebuilt. During the Klondike gold rush of 1897, Seattle became a bustling supply center for prospectors heading north. Salmon fishing and lumbering, apple growing and the aircraft industry, have all played a part in Washington State's economic development.

---

**Question**: Which of Washington's volcanic peaks erupted in 1980, sending smoke and ash twelve miles into the air?

**Answer**: Mount St. Helens, in the Cascade Range. A tremendous explosion took place at 8:32 A.M. on May 18. Over thirteen hundred feet of the mountaintop was blown off, reducing Mount St. Helens from ninety-six hundred feet to eighty-three hundred feet.

---

# Asa Mercer, Matchmaker

"I am in need of a wife. . . ." So began a letter written by a man from the Territory of Washington to the famous Chicago mail-order house Montgomery Ward sometime in the 1870s. As the company's catalogue advertised just about everything a person could want, the writer—a lonely bachelor— assumed he could order a bride by mail as well. He asked for "a good wife . . . weight 150 pounds . . . either fair or dark," and described himself as being "45 years old" with "black hair and blue eyes," and owning "quite a lot of stock and land."

The kindly Mr. Aaron Montgomery Ward wrote back. His company didn't offer wives, he explained, and it probably wasn't even a very good idea to order a bride by mail. But once the man did find a wife, Mr. Ward assured him, the company would be happy to supply her with "wearing apparel or household goods," or anything else she might need.

The lonely stock raiser from the Washington Territory was hardly unusual. All over the frontier communities of the West, loggers and miners, farmers and fishermen, were suffering from the scarcity of women. They wanted companionship, marriage, and families. But how did a lone man persuade a young woman of good background to travel to the pioneering world of the Pacific Northwest to marry someone she had never seen before? It took the talents of an enterprising matchmaker to arrange all the details of such an undertaking.

For a brief time during the 1860s, such a matchmaker had appeared in the person of a young man named Asa Shinn Mercer. Asa Mercer first arrived in Seattle to join his older brother, Judge Thomas Mercer. Still in his early twenties, and a recent graduate of Franklin College in Ohio, Asa Mercer soon found himself teaching school at Seattle's Territorial University, which had opened in 1861. As nobody in the then tiny community of Seattle had enough education to enter college, Mercer taught reading, writing, and arithmetic to unschooled loggers. And as the only qualified teacher, he was also named university president!

People laughed, but Mercer pressed on. He increased enrollment by recruiting students from backwoods settlements and built the first dormitory of what was later to become the University of Washington. By 1863, however, he had come up with a new promotional idea for the Washington Territory. The nation was in the midst of the Civil War and, if anything, even fewer unmarried women were venturing away from home. Yet the war had created a severe shortage of men back East. Asa Mercer reasoned that if he could get the territorial legislature to sponsor a trip to Boston, he'd be able to bring back a boatload of young women of good character willing to marry and raise families on the new frontier.

The legislature agreed that Asa Mercer's idea was an excellent one, but it turned down his request for money. So with some of his own funds and whatever he could borrow from Seattle's willing bachelors, Mercer made the long ocean voyage around the tip of South America to Boston. Mercer was tall and distinguished looking, with a straightforward manner and an impressive beard. And he *had* been a university president. The families of the young women were nevertheless concerned about entrusting their daughters to a five-month sea journey of over thirteen thousand miles in the company of an unknown young man. Moreover, Mercer had just about run out of money, so each young woman would have to pay two hundred dollars for her passage.

Mercer had hoped to bring home fifty young brides, but he was lucky to find eleven willing to make the journey. These brave and spirited young women ranged in age from fifteen to twenty-five. They disembarked at Seattle on May 16, 1864, and were greeted enthusiastically by the whole town—including the marriage-minded bachelors, all spruced up and dressed in their best. The Seattle *Gazette* wrote a column praising and thanking "Mr. Mercer for his efforts in encouraging this much needed kind of immigration," and suggesting that he promptly be elected to the territorial legislature, which he was—unanimously.

The success of Asa Mercer's matchmaking mission led quite soon to a repeat visit to the East. This time he was armed with letters of recommendation from several of the Mercer Girls, as the newly married young women were now known. In addition, he was quite well supplied with funds, for he had signed contracts with a number of Seattle bachelors. Each of them had paid three hundred dollars in advance for "a suitable wife of good moral character and reputation" to arrive in Seattle "on or before September, 1865." This sum was to cover the cost of the young woman's passage plus a portion of Mercer's expenses.

On this trip Asa Mercer planned to see President Abraham Lincoln first thing on his arrival in the East. He hoped the president would make a public statement suggesting that marriagable young women who'd been widowed or orphaned by the brutal war should consider making new lives in the Pacific Northwest. Such a suggestion would help his cause immensely.

To Mercer's shock and despair, he arrived in Washington, D.C., to find the city hushed and saddened. Just days earlier, on the evening of April 14, 1865, President Lincoln had been shot. He had died early the next morning. The government was paralyzed, and no one would see Mercer.

Months dragged by, and even Mercer's hopes of borrowing a United States Navy vessel to transport his brides to Seattle came to nothing. He had dreamed of delivering five hundred future wives to the West, and he might have if all had gone according to plan. As he searched for a private vessel, many likely young women grew tired of waiting. When he finally sailed, he had fewer than a hundred in the group.

In April 1866, the ship docked in San Francisco and new troubles arose. The captain refused to go on to Seattle. Some of the young women received offers of marriage from San Francisco bachelors and chose to remain there. Finally Mercer managed to raise the funds to transport the remaining Mercer Girls to Seattle. Some reports say there were forty-six brides among the late arrivals; others say fifty-seven. In any case, most of the young women whose passage had been paid for were delivered to the waiting bachelors. And Asa Mercer himself had found a bride in the course of the journey. She was Annie E. Stephens, the daughter of a hatmaker from Philadelphia.

Asa Mercer had done his best for the Washington Territory he had come to love and admire. But the risks of long-distance matchmaking were dangerous and burdensome. Also, he began to find himself in the middle of husband-wife disputes among some of the Seattle couples he had helped put together. So in 1867 Asa and Annie took themselves off to Oregon, later Texas, and finally Wyoming, where Mercer became involved in newspaper publishing and cattle ranching.

Some people would always find it funny that he'd once been president of a university that taught grammar-school subjects to lumbermen, or that he'd spent years at sea and in East Coast cities trying to populate the West. But Asa Mercer *had* succeeded in no small way. His Territorial University became the first-rate University of Washington. And there are people in the state of Washington today who can proudly boast that great-grandma was a Mercer Girl.

# WEST VIRGINIA

West Virginia takes its name from Virginia, of which it was a part until the Civil War. Its nickname, *The Mountain State,* partly explains the reason for its separation. The Appalachian Mountains of West Virginia formed a natural barrier beyond which life was very different from that in the rest of Virginia. There was no large-scale farming in the west, and very few slaves were owned. With the outbreak of the Civil War, in 1861, the West Virginia region sided with the North and refused to recognize Virginia's secession from the Union. By an overwhelming popular vote, it set up its own capital at Wheeling. West Virginia became a state of the Union on June 20, 1863.

The first Europeans in the region broke through the mountains in the late 1600s to find themselves in the hunting grounds of the Cherokee, Shawnee, and other Indian peoples. In the 1700s settlers of Welsh, Scots-Irish, and German background arrived and took up small-scale farming in the mountain valleys.

Deposits of coal, first discovered in 1742, are thought to lie beneath more than half of West Virginia.

After railroads expanded into the area, in the mid-1800s, West Virginia became "the coal bin of the world." But the long hours, unhealthy working conditions, and low wages of the miners were to lead to many years of intense labor strife. Other natural resources include brine-pool salts that have become the foundation of a chemical-manufacturing industry, and sands and clays from which glassware and pottery are made.

---

**Question**: Can you think of an answer to this riddle? What was the greatest feat of strength ever performed in the United States?

**Answer**: Wheeling West Virginia

---

# Mother Jones, the Coal Miners' Angel

Mother Jones, "the coal miners' angel," was also known as "the most dangerous woman in America." Who was she, and how could she be loved and admired by some, yet hated and feared by others?

Her real name was Mary Harris Jones and, in the 1890s, when she first appeared in the coal-mining country of West Virginia, she was already in her late sixties. This small, rounded, white-haired woman had a sweet but sharp-featured face and blue eyes that seemed to pierce right through her spectacles. She dressed sedately in black and always wore a hat or bonnet. She looked like a schoolmistress and, in fact, in her younger days she had been one.

Mary Harris was born in a one-room cottage in County Cork, Ireland, the child of a poor family that worked at tenant farming on a large estate. She gave the date of her birth as May 1, 1830. Her grandfather was hanged for taking part in a peasant rebellion and in 1835 her father fled to America. Mary, her mother, and her two brothers joined him in Toronto, Canada, several years later. Although she was a laborer's child, Mary Harris managed to graduate from high school and receive some teacher training. After that she was on her own. She taught school in Maine, in Michigan, and in Memphis, Tennessee. There she met George Jones, an ironworker, whom she married in 1861.

The life of Mary Harris Jones might have passed unnoticed and in quiet contentment if not for two disastrous events that changed her future around. In 1867, her four little children—three girls and a boy—*and* her husband all died within a few weeks during the yellow fever epidemic that swept Memphis. Soon afterward the widowed and childless Mary made her way to Chicago,

COMPANY HOUSES
AND BREAKER BOYS

where she opened a dressmaking shop. Four years later, she lost everything she owned in the Great Chicago Fire of 1871.

Wandering about among the many left homeless by the fire, Mary began to attend the meetings of a recently formed labor organization. Ever since the Civil War, newly built rail lines and newer and bigger industries had been springing up all over America. There were fortunes to be made from railroad building, iron foundries, steel mills, coal and copper mines, and textile and garment factories.

But these fortunes rested on the labor of immigrants, emancipated blacks, and other poor and desperate members of the working class, including children as young as nine or ten. As Mary later wrote in her autobiography, the Civil War had put an end to one "brutal form of slavery" only to give rise to another—"industrial slavery."

Soon Mary was out among the country's working people, making speeches, giving encouragement, and even scolding them to get them to organize for better pay and working conditions and shorter hours. In those early years of the labor movement, people worked twelve, fourteen, and even sixteen hours a day, six days a week. The average wage of a West Virginia coal miner was $275 a year.

Although West Virginia had the richest coal mines in the country, it had the worst-paid workers. They and their families were housed in shacks on the mountainsides. They lived in "company towns" where everything was owned by the mining companies—the houses, the general store, the school, the church, even the funeral parlor. They were paid in paper certificates called scrip instead of in real money. Food and other necessities had to be bought at the company store, where prices were always higher than anywhere else. Other stores wouldn't accept the coal company's scrip. Often the miners were so deep in debt, they never saw any scrip at all on payday.

Conditions in the mines themselves were extremely unhealthy and dangerous. Men and boys worked with picks and shovels in narrow, damp tunnels. Cave-ins maimed them for life or buried them alive. Explosions, too, were a serious threat, for a tiny spark could ignite the gases released when the coal was dug. Young children worked as "breaker boys," sorting pieces of slate from the coal as it poured out of the mine in chutes. A sleepy or inattentive boy was struck hard across the knuckles with a stick by the breaker boss.

Imagine the surprise of the West Virginia coal miners when, awaiting the visit of a representative of the recently formed United Mine Workers, they watched a small, black-clad woman climb down from the train and announce herself as "Mother" Jones. Union work was highly dangerous. The police, the courts, the local governments, and the newspapers were all on the side—and often in the pay—of the coal bosses, who also employed armed guards of their own. No woman had ever attempted to rally the workers and lead them in the brutal strikes, which frequently led to bloodshed.

Yet the miners listened raptly to Mother Jones. She was feisty and tough, and she didn't shrink from calling the mine owners "high-class burglars." When company guards chased her, she met with the miners in the woods at night, in barns, or even in abandoned mines. She was arrested at least twice in West Virginia, once in 1902 for defying a court order forbidding her to hold a meeting. Another time, in 1913, she was accused of planning to steal a machine gun and blow up a train.

Although she was then eighty-three years old, Mother Jones was jailed for nearly three months. She developed pneumonia and was almost gleeful at the possibility that she would die in jail. The whole country would then learn about the spies and gunmen of the West Virginia mine owners, about the jailings and murders of those workers who stood up for the union, and about the strikebreakers, or "scabs," the company brought in to replace them.

As it turned out, Mother Jones didn't die in jail. In fact, she lived past her hundredth birthday and died in bed, on November 30, 1930. Her 1913 imprisonment in West Virginia *had* accomplished some of her goals. Through the efforts of the governor, the coal companies and the union got together and agreed on a shorter working day, pay envelopes twice a month instead of once, and the opportunity for miners to shop at any store they wished.

Although the struggle for ongoing and permanent improvements in the mines was to continue beyond her lifetime, Mother Jones would always be remembered for her fight on behalf of the toilworn and the downtrodden. Having lost her own children, this fearless woman became a mother to all those who would raise their voices to demand a fairer share of the fruits of their labor.

Even today the verses of this popular folk song lamenting her death are recalled in the mountains of West Virginia:

*The world today is mourning*
*The death of Mother Jones.*
*Grief and sorrow hover*
*Around the miners' homes.*

*This grand old champion of labor*
*Has gone to a better land.*
*But the hardworking miners,*
*They miss her guiding hand.*

MOTHER JONES IN 1925

# WISCONSIN

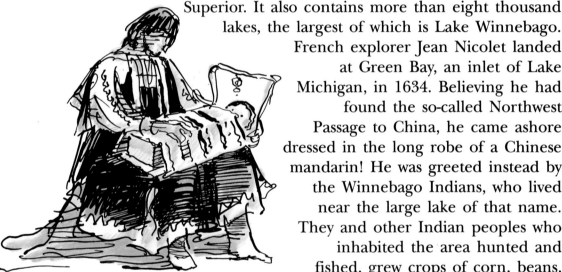

**W**isconsin may owe its name to *ouisconsin,* a French pronunciation of a Chippewa Indian word for "gathering of the waters." Wisconsin has shorelines on two of the Great Lakes, Michigan and Superior. It also contains more than eight thousand lakes, the largest of which is Lake Winnebago. French explorer Jean Nicolet landed at Green Bay, an inlet of Lake Michigan, in 1634. Believing he had found the so-called Northwest Passage to China, he came ashore dressed in the long robe of a Chinese mandarin! He was greeted instead by the Winnebago Indians, who lived near the large lake of that name. They and other Indian peoples who inhabited the area hunted and fished, grew crops of corn, beans, and squash, and gathered wild rice from the lakeshores.

### CHIPPEWA MOTHER AND CHILD

The French and, later, the British claimed the territory, which they valued mainly for fur trapping. It passed into American hands after the American Revolution. Wisconsin became a state of the Union on May 29, 1848. By that time lead mining was of major importance. Wisconsin's nickname, *The Badger State,* comes from the lead miners' practice of making temporary cavelike homes in the hillsides. The caves looked like the burrows made by badgers. Many of the miners were from Cornwall, in southwestern England. Other immigrant groups, especially the Germans, developed the dairying and beer-brewing industries that made Wisconsin famous.

**Question**: Where and when in the United States was the first kindergarten class held?

**Answer**: In Watertown, Wisconsin, in 1856. The nation's first kindergarten (German for "children's garden") was started by Margaretha Meyer Schurz, wife of the abolitionist Carl Schurz. Her kindergarten was for the children of German-speaking immigrants.

# The Ringling Brothers Start a Circus

"Our first performance . . . was an exhibition of 'stage fright.' " This was how Charles Ringling, of the famous Ringling Brothers Circus, described putting on a show for the first time in his life. "At the sight of the audience" Ringling and his brothers suffered from "trembling knees," and their "teeth fairly chattered."

What *were* the five Rüngeling boys (who had changed their name to Ringling) doing on a stage anyhow? They were the sons of a German harness maker who lived in a woodframe house in the tiny town of Baraboo, in southern Wisconsin. Baraboo, by the way, had also changed its name. It had once been called Baribault, after a Frenchman who'd started a trading post there in the early 1800s.

Now the year was 1882, and somehow the Ringling boys saw a future for themselves in something quite different from harness and saddle making. They had formed a little troupe of clowns and jugglers who also performed jokes, skits, and musical numbers. Albert, the oldest, was thirty. Otto was twenty-four. Alfred was twenty, Charles eighteen, and John sixteen. There were also two other brothers in the family who weren't as directly involved, and a sister.

The five performing Ringlings decided to call their troupe the Ringling Bros. Classic and Comic Concert Company. But they were too frightened to give their first performance in their home town of Baraboo, where everyone would laugh at them if they flopped. So they opened instead in the even smaller town of Mazomanie, Wisconsin, twenty-five miles southwest of Baraboo.

On Monday afternoon, November 27, they started out bravely with a parade through little Mazomanie. All the Ringlings played musical instruments, from the violin to the cornet, from the trombone to the big bass drum, and the parade was a way of drawing people's attention to the performance that evening.

The idea of going into the amusement business had come to Albert Ringling back in May 1870, when he'd seen such a parade just across the Wisconsin state line in Iowa. It was given by the Dan Rice Circus, which cruised the Mississippi River on a showboat. After Albert and some of his younger brothers attended the show, the circus stars never left their eyes.

But now, on the great day of their own opening, everything seemed to go wrong for the Ringlings. First off, two youths from Mazomanie recognized them and, by curtain time, the whole town knew that they were just a group of amateurs from Baraboo who'd never been on a stage before. The paid audience consisted of only fifty-two people, and the ticket sales, at twenty-five cents each, came to thirteen dollars. The boys owed six dollars to August Schmitz, the owner of the theater, which left them with too little money to continue their planned tour of one-night stands in small towns through western Wisconsin and eastern Iowa. It looked like the Ringlings' career in show business was finished even before it started!

The boys were so eager and earnest, though, that Mr. Schmitz took a liking to them. He reduced the rent, enabling them to get back on the road and head for the next town on their tour. Forever afterward the Ringlings remembered August Schmitz's kindness and saw to it that he and his family got free tickets to their circus whenever it played near Mazomanie.

After that scary beginning, the Ringlings' luck changed. The very next night, at a Wisconsin town called Spring Green, the hall was filled to capacity by young people from the countryside who'd mistakenly thought there was going to be a dance there. They stayed to laugh at the comedy sketches and cheer the acrobatics, and the Ringlings' share of the ticket sales came to ninety dollars.

Right through to the third of February, 1883, the Classic and Comic Concert Company slogged through winter snows and battled bitter winds, dragging its props, scenery, and musical instruments over bumpy roads in wagons drawn by horses rented from local farmers. That summer the boys worked in other small circuses to gain more experience. Then they set out on another tour in the fall and winter of 1883–84. They renamed their show the Ringling Bros. Grand Carnival of Fun and played the lumber camps of northern Wisconsin. The lonely loggers were thrilled to have some entertainment. With a thousand dollars saved from their two long, hard stints on the road, the Ringlings were at last ready to open a circus in Baraboo, on May 19, 1884.

Today when we think of a circus, we see tigers jumping through flaming hoops, heart-stopping high-wire acts, bareback riders on dancing horses, and of course elephants. But the Ringling Brothers circus that was at last ready to play its hometown of Baraboo had none of these attractions. Aside from an "educated" pet pig and some snakes, it was made up mainly of tumblers and contortionists, balancing acts, magicians, fire-eaters, and band music.

The five brothers worked at the tent rigging, the publicity, the parade, and the entertainment. Albert's wife sewed the costumes and doubled as a snake charmer. The entire staff was only twenty-four people. But the big tent could hold six hundred, and it was pretty well filled for both the afternoon and evening shows.

Most towns were so small in the 1880s that two performances were enough to cover the show-going population. So the very next day the Ringlings started a five-week wagon tour of one-day appearances. Just as with their winter tours (when they had at least been able to play indoors), the going was rough. Frequent thunderstorms that summer of 1884 made roads impassable and turned circus-tent lots into seas of mud. Hail fell and tornadoes threatened. But the Ringlings pushed on. Even though profits were small, the pleasure the Ringlings brought to entertainment-starved people was rewarding. And Albert, who still dreamed of a really great circus, kept everybody's spirit up.

Little by little the Ringlings expanded. In 1890 they bought seventeen railway cars and put their show on rails, taking it to many more towns and cities in the Midwest. They also acquired real circus animals—lions, elephants, performing horses—and hired professional acts from other circuses, which gradually shrank as theirs grew bigger.

The brothers gave up performing and took on supervisory jobs full-time. Albert produced and directed. Otto became treasurer. Alfred did public relations, Charles did the outdoor advertising, and John took care of the railroad routing. The other two brothers pitched in too. August took over the advance publicity and Henry managed the ticket office. It was lucky there were so *many* Ringlings, *and* that they got on so well.

No wonder that by the early 1900s the Ringling Brothers Circus, known throughout the Midwest, was ready to take on the Barnum and Bailey Circus, which was famous in the East. The two giants met in 1904, when James A. Bailey took the bold step of bringing *his* circus to Madison, Wisconsin. (Phineas T. Barnum, Bailey's partner, had died in 1891.)

The Ringlings eyed Mr. Bailey with deep suspicion at first. But finally it was agreed that the two circuses would divide the territory and keep the peace. A few years later, when James Bailey died, the Ringlings bought the Barnum and Bailey show, and in 1919 they merged the two into the Ringling Bros. and Barnum & Bailey Combined Shows. It was now truly "The Greatest Show on Earth."

Today all of the five Ringling Brothers who started the great circus are gone. John, the last of them, died in 1936. But back in Baraboo, which was the Ringlings' winter quarters from 1884 to 1918, they are not forgotten. The State Historical Society of Wisconsin now runs a Circus World Museum there. The museum, with its big top, parades, and band concerts, re-creates the history of the American circus. It celebrates the hard work and dedication of the Ringling Brothers, which grew out of the pure joy of providing fun—and began with a pet pig, a juggler, and a dream.

# WYOMING

"Wyoming" sounds like a word that might have come from one of the Indian languages of the West. Actually, it's a Delaware Indian word from Pennsylvania, where there is a Wyoming Valley. The name was first suggested for the Wyoming Territory by a congressman from Ohio. Its meaning—"upon the great plain"—describes the Great Plains in the eastern half of Wyoming. The Rocky Mountains rise in the western half of the state as a series of jagged, snow-capped peaks.

Crow, Blackfoot, Sioux, and Cheyenne Indians occupied the plains when the first explorers and fur trappers entered the area, in the 1700s. Part of the region became a United States possession through the Louisiana Purchase of 1803. But the population grew slowly throughout the 1800s. Pioneers heading for Utah, Oregon, and California saw little there

CHEYENNE CHIEF

in the way of promising farmland. In the late 1860s, though, the coming of the railroads helped give rise to large-scale cattle and sheep raising.

In 1869, while it was still a territory, Wyoming's legislature gave women the right to vote, the first governing body to do so since the nation was formed. For this reason Wyoming is nicknamed *The Equality State*. Wyoming joined the Union on July 10, 1890. Economic growth followed as oil and coal reserves were developed. Tourism is a major industry, with visitors drawn to world-famous

280

Yellowstone and Grand Teton national parks, as well as other scenic wonders and sporting attractions.

> **Question**: How did Old Faithful, in Wyoming's Yellowstone National Park, get its name?
>
> **Answer**: Since its discovery in 1870, the geyser known as Old Faithful has shot a column of water about one hundred fifty feet high into the air roughly every hour. The temperature of the steaming water is just below boiling point, and the display lasts for around four minutes each time.

# Where Women Came First

Esther Hobart Morris arrived in South Pass City, Wyoming, in 1869, a very angry woman. She was six feet tall and weighed two hundred pounds, so she was not somebody to be trifled with. What had made Esther Morris so mad?

Well, for one thing, her first husband had died a while back in Illinois, and she'd found herself unable to inherit his estate because she was a woman. She felt that just wasn't fair. Women had been denied legal and political rights almost everywhere in the world for a very long time. Even in the United States women were not allowed to vote, hold public office, or sit on juries. And in many places they were deprived of the right to own property or manage money.

Something else had fired up Esther Morris's fighting spirit. Back in Illinois she'd heard a speech by Susan B. Anthony, the famous fighter for women's suffrage, the right to vote. Anthony spoke about the injustice of the proposed Fifteenth Amendment to the United States Constitution. This amendment dealt with the right to vote of the newly freed slaves, following the Civil War. It stated that no person should be denied that right because of race or color or having been in servitude. That was fine, as far as it went. The trouble was, it said nothing about the equality of the sexes. After the Fifteenth Amendment became law, there would *still* be no federal law assuring women—of *any* race or color—of *their* right to vote. And not a single state or territory permitted women's suffrage.

South Pass City in 1869 hardly seemed the sort of place to start a suffrage campaign. It was a tiny spot in the mountains that had become a boom town after the discovery of gold a couple of years before. Esther Morris went there to join her second husband, John, and her three grown sons, who had arrived earlier to try their fortunes. The entire population was not much over a thousand, and women were even scarcer than gold nuggets.

Oddly enough, though, Esther Morris found somebody among her new neighbors who agreed with her about the importance of giving women the vote. He was William H. Bright, a forty-six-year-old miner who also kept a saloon in South Pass City. Bright didn't have much education, but he had a wife named Julia who was twenty-one years younger than he. Julia, who was better educated than her husband, wanted the vote, and William Bright agreed. He reasoned that, if it became known that Wyoming offered equal rights for women, a lot more women would come to the Territory. And that would be all to the good.

So with Esther Morris's enthusiastic support, Bright introduced a women's voting-rights bill into the upper house of the Territorial Legislature. It was November 1869, and the measure was quickly passed, possibly out of respect for Bright, who also happened to be president of the upper house.

The bill then went to the lower house of the legislature. There things went very differently. The all-male representatives of the people of the Wyoming Territory took one look at it and began to laugh. They thought that giving women the vote was the funniest thing they'd ever heard. Jokes were tossed back and forth across the chamber. Why not adjourn right now? Why not put off the vote until next July fourth (when, of course, the legislature wouldn't be in session)? Just imagine women making up their minds long enough to cast a ballot? Should the vote be given to all women, or just to "ladies"? These and other belittling comments kept the men in an uproar.

Then somebody in the lower house came up with an idea. The entire Territorial Legislature was made up of members of the Democratic Party. But the newly appointed governor of the Wyoming Territory, who'd been named by President Ulysses S. Grant, was a Republican. He was sure to veto any bill the Democrats approved. So why not pass the measure just for a lark?

JULIA AND WM. BRIGHT

A few members still held back, but most were in favor of the joke. By a margin of six to four, they decreed that all women of the Wyoming Territory over the age of twenty-one should be given the right to vote and to hold office. Then the bill went to Governor John Campbell's desk for the expected veto.

Governor Campbell was a young man, but he wasn't stupid. He felt that he should respond to what the people of the Territory seemed to want. Also, he didn't want to put the Republican Party in a bad light. So on December 10, 1869, he signed the bill into law! The members of the lower house were shocked, but there wasn't a thing they could do about it. The joke had turned out to be on them.

Their only consolation was that in 1869 there were fewer than a thousand voting-age females in the Wyoming Territory, as against six thousand males. But that proportion would gradually change, as word got out that Wyoming was the only place in the United States where a woman had the same political rights as a man. A much more immediate change took place in Wyoming in February 1870, when the first female judge was appointed in South Pass City. She was none other than Esther Hobart Morris.

Throughout her term on the bench, the fifty-six-year-old Mrs. Morris ran her courtroom from the parlor of her log cabin. She kept careful records of all the proceedings of her court and was known as a fair and competent judge, despite her lack of legal training. Even arguing lawyers listened when she pounded her gavel and ordered, "Boys, behave yourselves!"

Women came first in Wyoming as jurors, too, as early as March 1870. And in 1925 Wyoming elected Nellie Tayloe Ross as governor. She was the first woman in the United States to hold that office.

Esther Hobart Morris died in 1902, too soon to know that a great honor would be paid her by the state of Wyoming. In 1960 a bronze statue of her took its place in Statuary Hall in the United States Capitol in Washington, D.C. She stands there proudly, one of a very few women among the heroic figures of the other states.

The inscription tells us that Wyoming chose her as its outstanding citizen because of her role in making it "The 1st Government of the World to Grant Women Equal Rights." If only she could have seen this tribute, Esther Morris might very well have dropped her fierce expression and smiled.

ESTHER MORRIS
STATUARY HALL
WASHINGTON, D.C.

# Bibliography

Adams, John R. *Harriet Beecher Stowe.* New York: Twayne Publishers, 1963.

Atkinson, Linda. *Mother Jones: The Most Dangerous Woman in America.* New York: Crown Publishers, 1978.

Bailey, Thomas A. *Probing America's Past: A Critical Examination of Major Myths and Misconceptions, Volume I.* Lexington, Massachusetts: D.C. Heath and Company, 1973.

——————. *Probing America's Past: A Critical Examination of Major Myths and Misconceptions, Volume II.* Lexington, Massachusetts: D.C. Heath and Company, 1973.

Boorstin, Daniel J. *The Americans: The Democratic Experience.* New York: Random House, 1973

——————. *The Americans: The National Experience.* New York: Random House, 1965.

Braathen, Sverre O. and Faye O. "Circus Monarchs: The Ringling Brothers." *Bandwagon,* May–June 1970.

Cable, Mary, and The Editors of American Heritage. *American Manners and Morals.* New York: American Heritage Publishing Company, 1969.

Campbell, Douglas G. "Saarinen's Triumphal Arch to Westward Expansion." *Journal of the West,* Volume 21, April 1982.

Carson, Gerald. *Cornflake Crusade.* New York: Rinehart and Company, Inc., 1957.

Cheney, Lynne. "It All Began in Wyoming." *American Heritage,* April 1973.

Corle, Edwin. *John Studebaker: An American Dream.* New York: E.P. Dutton, 1948.

Durham, Michael S. *The Smithsonian Guide to Historic America: The Mid-Atlantic States.* New York: Stewart, Tabori and Chang, 1989.

Editors of Time-Life Books. *This Fabulous Century: 1870–1900.* Alexandria, Virginia: Time-Life Books, Inc., 1970. Revised edition, 1985.

Elliot, Maud Howe, and Florence Howe Hall. *Laura Bridgman: Dr. Howe's Famous Pupil and What He Taught Her.* Boston: Little, Brown, 1903.

Erdoes, Richard. *Saloons of the Old West.* New York: Knopf, 1979.

Fetherling, Dale. *Mother Jones, The Miners' Angel: A Portrait.* Carbondale, Illinois: Southern Illinois University Press, 1974.

Furer, Howard B., editor. *The Scandinavians in America: 986–1970.* Dobbs Ferry, New York: Oceana Publications, Inc., 1972.

Gwaltney, Francis Irby. "A Survey of Historic Washington, Arkansas." *Arkansas Historical Quarterly*, Volume XVII, Winter 1958.

Hoffman, Velma Rudd. "Lt. Beale and the Camel Caravans through Arizona." *Arizona Highways*, October 1957.

Hudson, Patricia L., and Sandra L. Ballard. *The Smithsonian Guide to Historic America: The Carolinas and the Appalachian States.* New York: Stewart, Tabori and Chang, 1989.

James, H.L. *Acoma: People of the White Rock.* West Chester, Pennsylvania: Schiffer Publishing Ltd., 1988.

Jones, Mother. *The Autobiography of Mother Jones.* Chicago: Charles H. Kerr Publishing Company, 1925. 1976 edition.

Lamb, Harold. *New Found World: How North America Was Discovered and Explored.* New York: Doubleday, 1955.

Langdon, William Chauncy. *Everyday Things in American Life 1776–1876.* New York: Charles Scribner's Sons, 1941.

Longstreet, Stephen. *A Century on Wheels: The Story of Studebaker.* New York: Henry Holt and Company, 1952.

McCunn, Ruthanne Lum. *Chinese-American Portraits: Personal Histories 1828–1988.* San Francisco: Chronicle Books, 1988.

Meltzer, Milton. *Mark Twain Himself.* New York: Thomas Y. Crowell, 1960.

Miller, Nathan. *F.D.R.: An Intimate History.* New York: Doubleday, 1983.

Morison, Samuel Eliot. *The European Discovery of America: The Northern Voyages, A.D. 500–1600.* New York: Oxford University Press, 1971.

Morris, Richard B., and James Woodress, editors. *Voices from America's Past, Volume 1: The Colonies and the New Nation.* New York: E.P. Dutton, 1961, 1963.

——————. *Voices from America's Past, Volume 2: Backwoods Democracy to World Power.* New York: E.P. Dutton, 1961, 1962, 1963.

——————. *Voices from America's Past, Volume 3: The Twentieth Century.* New York: E.P. Dutton, 1962, 1963.

Nichols, David, editor. *Ernie's America: The Best of Ernie Pyle's 1930s Travel Dispatches.* New York: Random House, 1989.

Ogburn, Charlton. *Railroads: The Great American Adventure.* Washington, D.C.: National Geographic Society, 1977.

Reinhardt, Richard, editor. *Workin' on the Railroad: Reminiscences from the Age of Steam.* Palo Alto, California: American West Publishing Company, 1970.

Rochlin, Harriet and Fred. *Pioneer Jews: A New Life in the Far West.* Boston: Houghton Mifflin Company, 1984.

Saxon, Lyle. *Lafitte the Pirate.* New York: The Century Company, 1930.

Schlissel, Lillian. *Women's Diaries of the Westward Journey.* New York: Schocken Books, 1982.

Shulsinger, Stephanie Cooper. "Asa Mercer, Pioneer Promoter." *Real West Magazine*, January 1970.

Thorp, Raymond, W. *Bowie Knife*. Albuquerque, New Mexico: University of New Mexico Press, 1948.

Ulrich, Laurel Thatcher. *A Midwife's Tale: The Life of Martha Ballard, Based on Her Diary, 1785–1812*. New York: Alfred A. Knopf, 1990.

Walker, Robert H. *Everyday Life in the Age of Enterprise, 1865–1900*. New York: G.P. Putnam's Sons, 1967.

Weatherford, Jack. *Indian Givers: How the Indians of the* ___ *ransformed the World*. New Y___

Wharton, David B. ___ ___ ___a University Press, ___

Wheeler, Bernadette. "Mississip___ ___8.

Wiencek, Henry. *The Smithso___ ital Region*. New Yor___

Winestine, Belle Fligel___ *Western History*, Sum___

Wright, Louis B. *Everyday L___ Sons, 1968.

Wright, Louis B. and Elaine ___ *1787–1860*. New York: G.P. Put___

Thorp, Raymond, W. *Bowie Knife.* Albuquerque, New Mexico: University of New Mexico Press, 1948.

Ulrich, Laurel Thatcher. *A Midwife's Tale: The Life of Martha Ballard, Based on Her Diary, 1785–1812.* New York: Alfred A. Knopf, 1990.

Walker, Robert H. *Everyday Life in the Age of Enterprise, 1865–1900.* New York: G.P. Putnam's Sons, 1967.

Weatherford, Jack. *Indian Givers: How the Indians of the Americas Transformed the World.* New Yo

Wharton, David B. Bloomington, India a: Indiana University Press, 1972.

Wheeler, Bernadette. "Mississippi Mud Pie (or Cake)." *Newsday,* July 13, 1988.

Wiencek, Henry. *The Smithsonian Guide to Historic America: Virginia and the Capital Region.* New York: Stewart, Tabori and Chang, 1989.

Winestine, Belle Fligelman. "Mother Was Shocked." *Montana: The Magazine of Western History,* Summer 1974.

Wright, Louis B. *Everyday Life on the American Frontier.* New York: G.P. Putnam's Sons, 1968.

Wright, Louis B. and Elaine W. Fowler. *Everyday Life in the New Nation 1787–1860.* New York: G.P. Putnam's Sons, 1972.

Gwaltney, Francis Irby. "A Survey of Historic Washington, Arkansas." *Arkansas Historical Quarterly*, Volume XVII, Winter 1958.

Hoffman, Velma Rudd. "Lt. Beale and the Camel Caravans through Arizona." *Arizona Highways*, October 1957.

Hudson, Patricia L., and Sandra L. Ballard. *The Smithsonian Guide to Historic America: The Carolinas and the Appalachian States*. New York: Stewart, Tabori and Chang, 1989.

James, H.L. *Acoma: People of the White Rock*. West Chester, Pennsylvania: Schiffer Publishing Ltd., 1988.

Jones, Mother. *The Autobiography of Mother Jones*. Chicago: Charles H. Kerr Publishing Company, 1925. 1976 edition.

Lamb, Harold. *New Found World: How North America Was Discovered and Explored*. New York: Doubleday, 1955.

Langdon, William Chauncy. *Everyday Things in American Life 1776–1876*. New York: Charles Scribner's Sons, 1941.

Longstreet, Stephen. *A Century on Wheels: The Story of Studebaker*. New York: Henry Holt and Company, 1952.

McCunn, Ruthanne Lum. *Chinese-American Portraits: Personal Histories 1828–1988*. San Francisco: Chronicle Books, 1988.

Meltzer, Milton. *Mark Twain Himself*. New York: Thomas Y. Crowell, 1960.

Miller, Nathan. *F.D.R.: An Intimate History*. New York: Doubleday, 1983.

Morison, Samuel Eliot. *The European Discovery of America: The Northern Voyages, A.D. 500–1600*. New York: Oxford University Press, 1971.

Morris, Richard B., and James Woodress, editors. *Voices from America's Past, Volume 1: The Colonies and the New Nation*. New York: E.P. Dutton, 1961, 1963.

——————. *Voices from America's Past, Volume 2: Backwoods Democracy to World Power*. New York: E.P. Dutton, 1961, 1962, 1963.

——————. *Voices from America's Past, Volume 3: The Twentieth Century*. New York: E.P. Dutton, 1962, 1963.

Nichols, David, editor. *Ernie's America: The Best of Ernie Pyle's 1930s Travel Dispatches*. New York: Random House, 1989.

Ogburn, Charlton. *Railroads: The Great American Adventure*. Washington, D.C.: National Geographic Society, 1977.

Reinhardt, Richard, editor. *Workin' on the Railroad: Reminiscences from the Age of Steam*. Palo Alto, California: American West Publishing Company, 1970.

Rochlin, Harriet and Fred. *Pioneer Jews: A New Life in the Far West*. Boston: Houghton Mifflin Company, 1984.

Saxon, Lyle. *Lafitte the Pirate*. New York: The Century Company, 1930.

Schlissel, Lillian. *Women's Diaries of the Westward Journey*. New York: Schocken Books, 1982.

Shulsinger, Stephanie Cooper. "Asa Mercer, Pioneer Promoter." *Real West Magazine*, January 1970.